SHADES OF BLUE

SHADES OF BLUE

US Naval Air Power Since 1941

Martin W. Bowman

Airlife
England

Dedication
This book is dedicated to the fond memory of
Roland H. Baker USN

'For I dipt into the future, far as the human eye could see,
Saw the Vision of the world, and all the wonder that would be;

Saw the heavens fill with commerce, argosies of magic sails,
Pilots of the purple twilight, dropping down with costly bales;

Heard the heavens fill with shouting, and there rain'd a ghastly dew
From the nation's airy navies grappling in the central blue . . .'

From *Locksley Hall* by Alfred Lord Tennyson

Copyright © 1999 Martin W. Bowman

First published in the UK in 1999
by Airlife Publishing Ltd

British Library Cataloguing-in-Publication Data
 A catalogue record for this book
 is available from the British Library

ISBN 1 84037 050 5

Typeset by Servis Filmsetting Ltd
Printed in Singapore

Airlife Publishing Ltd
101 Longden Road, Shrewsbury, SY3 9EB, England
E-mail: airlife@airlifebooks.com
Website: www.airlifebooks.com

Previous page: The last SB2C-5
BuNo83589 Helldiver restored by
the West Texas Wing of the
Confederate Air Force. First flight
on 27 September 1988 after re-build
to airworthiness after an accident at
Harlingen. (*Colonel Ted Short, CAF,
via Peter C. Smith*)

Opposite: Kermit Weeks in his
Eastern Aircraft Division FM-2
Wildcat BuNo86956 (N222FM) in
the colours of VC-12 over his
Fantasy of Flight Museum in Polk
County, Florida. (*Ed Toth*)

CONTENTS

ACKNOWLEDGEMENTS

The author would like to thank: Evan Adams; Lt-Cdr David J. Albritton USN; Richard E. Bagg; Mike Bailey; the late Roland H. Baker; the Confederate Air Force; Lt-Cdr Brent D. Chénard USN, and all the Public Affairs officers aboard *John F. Kennedy*; Lee Cook; Robert Cressman; Bill Crump; Dept of the Navy–Pentagon; Graham Dinsdale; Abe Dolim; Captain Edward J. Fahy Jr, and the crew of the USS *John F. Kennedy*; Thomas J. Fitton; Bob Gaines; Lt Christopher J. Madden USN; Gary Madgwick; McDonnell Douglas; Hunter Reinburg; Mike Rondot; Group Capt. Dave Roome; Roger Seybel, Northrop Grumman; Captain Armistead Smith USN Retd; Peter C. Smith; Tom Smith; Brynell Somerville; Ed Toth; Henrietta Wright, Dept of the Navy–Pentagon.

Thanks also go to the dedicated staff of the US 2nd Air Division Memorial Library in Norwich; Derek S. Hills, Trust Librarian; Linda J. Berube, American Fulbright Librarian; Lesley Fleetwood; and Christine Snowden, all of whom were most helpful and who provided much willing assistance with research.

(Photo: Roland H. Baker)

INTRODUCTION

When the *G. W. Parke Curtis*, a coal barge converted to transport and tow observation balloons, appeared during the American Civil War in November 1861 with General McClellan's Army of the Potomac, no one could possibly have foreseen just how important to the nation aircraft carriers would become, not just for the protection of the United States, but for the projection of American power around the globe.

Generations later, in 1941, US intervention in World War Two witnessed an unleashing of maritime power never before seen in history. Predictably, the Japanese attack on Pearl Harbor on 7 December awakened the sleeping giant that Fleet Admiral Isoroku Yamamoto, Japanese Commander-in-Chief and architect of the strike on Hawaii, had feared. Although four of the seven US carriers were lost in action in the first twelve months of the conflict, they were progressively replaced by seventeen larger and much more powerful Essex-class carriers, nine light carriers (CVLs) and 120 small deck escort carriers (CVEs). In several major battles at sea – starting with the Coral Sea on 7–9 May 1942 (the first naval battle fought entirely between aircraft), then Midway, Guadalcanal, and the Marianas – the Navy gradually imposed total air superiority over her enemy, and by 1945 had almost completely annihilated the Imperial Japanese Navy.

Post-war, developments came thick and fast. On 19 July 1946 the McDonnell XFD-1 prototype Phantom became the first US pure-jet landing aboard an aircraft carrier when it landed on the USS *Franklin D. Roosevelt*. In March 1948 the FJ-1 Fury became the first USN jet fighter to go to sea under operational conditions. In the Korean War, 1950–3, the F9F-2 Panther became the first USN jet fighter to take part in air combat. In 1954, the F11F-1 Tiger became the first supersonic operational carrier-borne naval

---

The Grumman F3F-2 and -3 were the last biplane fighters built in the US (1937–9). All F3F-2s (0968–1048) equipped the USMC, except eighteen for the US Navy's Fighting Squadron 6. F3Fs remained aboard carriers until June 1941. (*Author*)

Above: Lockheed-Vega PV-2 Harpoon *Fat Cat Too* belonging to the Combat Aircraft Museum at Lafayette, Louisiana. Powered by two air-cooled eighteen-cylinder Pratt & Whitney R-2800-31 Twin Row radials, each developing 2,000hp take-off power, PV-2s carried up to nine .50 calibre fixed machine-guns in the nose, two in a Martin top power turret, and two .30 calibre guns in the rear of the porcine fuselage. With machine-gun fire converging at 1,200ft range, an experienced pilot could cut a small ship in two. (*Author*)

interceptor in the world. In February 1958, the USS *Enterprise*, the world's second nuclear-powered surface warship, powered by eight reactors, was laid down. She was commissioned in November 1961.

Carriers and their air wings were in action throughout the Vietnam War, and operations reached their peak in May 1972 when almost 7,250 sorties were flown at a time when six carriers – the most on line in the conflict – were operating in the Gulf of Tonkin. During 'Linebacker I', which ended in October 1972, just over 23,650 sorties were flown against North Vietnam. 'Linebacker II', during which the Navy again contributed six air wings, succeeded in speeding up the peace talks, and a ceasefire came into effect on 27 January 1973. Two years later, in May 1975, the USN airlifted US nationals and personnel from Saigon in Operation 'Frequent Wind'.

By the mid-1980s the Navy had in service twelve carrier air wings aboard the same number of carriers. Each air wing could muster eighty or more aircraft. By 1992, fourteen carriers were in service, and a fifteenth, *Forrestal*, was in use as a training carrier. In 1990, the commissioning of the last two Nimitz-class nuclear-powered multi-role carriers took place. The

ten Nimitz-class carriers built and under construction are powered by two nuclear reactors and they do not need to refuel for more than a decade.

Operationally, the Navy has four carrier groups in the Pacific and four in the Atlantic. In 1990 'Desert Shield' saw a massive build-up of coalition forces, and six US carriers, two of them nuclear-powered, were deployed. During 'Desert Storm', these half dozen carriers between them dispatched over 20,900 sorties and dropped more than 12,250 tons of bombs. From a technical and operational standpoint, the Gulf War showed that America's military omnipotence could establish air superiority wherever it wished. In the absence of the Soviet Union as a competitor, there is no real challenger to American military aviation. Given the political will in times of crisis, the USN, should it choose, will deploy its sea- and airpower however it wants.

As we move into the new millennium, tailhooker crews will still be needed, but it is wholly unlikely that they will ever again duel in aerial dog-fighting to a degree which in the past fifty-six years has involved Wildcat and Zero, Panther Jet, Phantom and MiG.

CHAPTER 1
SHADES OF BLUE

At 0755 hours on the peaceful early morning of Sunday, 7 December 1941, the first wave of a Japanese strike force, some 350 aircraft in all, from their carriers 275 miles away reached the island of Oahu in the Hawaiian Islands, split into elements and headed for their objectives: Admiral Kimmel's American Pacific fleet at anchor in Pearl Harbor, and airfields nearby. America had broken the Japanese 'Purple Code' and knew that Japan was preparing for war, but had expected that the first bombs would fall on the Philippines or Malaya. When trainee radar operators on a rudimentary set at Opana, north of Pearl Harbor, reported many aircraft approaching, the Hawaiian Department, commanded by Lt-General Walter C. Short, interpreted these to be some B-17 Flying Fortresses which were expected, and the radar operators were ordered to stand down.

Personnel were forced to dive for cover as Mitsubishi A6M2 'Zero-Sen' fighters roared over the island at low level, machine-gunning aircraft parked at Wheeler Field, Kanaohe, Hickham and Ewa, while Nakajima B5N2 'Kate' torpedo-bombers attacked Battleship Row and achieved complete surprise. High-level bombers pounded Hickham Field, while Aichi D3A2 'Val' dive-bombers bombed Battleship Row. In the second attack, on Kanaohe, Pearl and Hickham, thirty-five fighters, seventy-eight dive-bombers and fifty-four high-level bombers added to the carnage.

Above: On 1 December the signal 'Niitaka Yama Nobore' ('Climb Mount Niitaka') announced that the attack was on, and at 0630 hours Hawaiian time on Sunday, 7 December, the first wave of Nagumo's striking force was launched. Here, an A6M Zero leaves the flight deck of the *Akagi* bound for Pearl Harbor. Altogether, six Imperial Japanese Navy fleet carriers took part in the operation. (*Abe Dolim*)

It was havoc. More than 2,000 sailors, soldiers and airmen, and a number of civilians, including some killed by 'friendly fire', perished in the two attacks. Within about twenty-five minutes four battleships had been sunk or destroyed, the *Arizona* exploding in a pall of smoke and flame and sinking upright to the bottom with more than 1,000 of her crew trapped below decks with no hope of escape. One battleship was damaged and ran aground, and three had relatively light damage.

Below: *TORA TORA TORA!* (the Japanese code-words meaning the 'surprise' was successful). Three Nakajima B5N2 'Kate' torpedo-bombers, photographed by one of the Japanese fliers, head for Pearl Harbor on 7 December. (*Abe Dolim*)

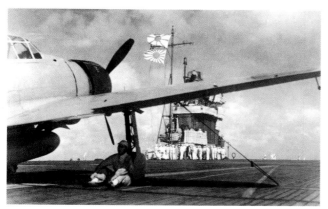

Above: Aboard the carrier *Akagi* (Red Castle), flagship of Vice-Admiral Chuichi Nagumo, commanding the Fast Carrier Striking Force, a crewman rests in the shade under the wing of a Mitsubishi A6M Zero-Sen ('Zeke') somewhere in the north Pacific, en route to the launching point for the attack on Pearl Harbor, Hawaii. On the night of 6 December 1941 Admiral Togo's battle-flag from the historic victory over the Russian fleet at Tsushima in 1905 was hoisted on the *Akagi*. (*Abe Dolim*)

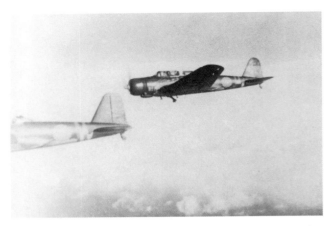

Above: Ford Island and Battleship Row burns, lower right, as Nakajima B5N2 'Kate' torpedo bombers leave Pearl Harbor after their attack.
(*Abe Dolim*)

Nineteen-year-old Abel L. Dolim, a machinist at the Hawaiian Pineapple Company, was returning from seven o'clock mass at St Patrick's to the family home in the Kaimuki district of Honolulu when he noticed white puffs of anti-aircraft shells over Pearl. No. 811 7th Avenue faced the harbor and was on high ground, so Abel witnessed the entire sequence of events from the front porch.

> I saw formations of high-level bombers – torpedo-type Nakajimas – about a dozen of them flying right over our house, heading north at about 8,000 feet I'd say. I was quite an aviation buff and built a lot of models when I was a kid. In fact, that's all I could think of – flying! I saw these white puffs over Pearl Harbor and I thought, 'What the heck's the Navy doing having gun practice on Sunday?' I was really surprised at that, so I

went in and turned on the radio set. Then I was really puzzled because KGMB was not on the air. A few minutes later a very excited announcer broke the silence and said, 'We are under sporadic attack by unknown airplanes.' I'll never forget he said 'sporadic'. Then he got really excited and I realised that something important had happened – that something was very wrong.

The Japanese had planned a follow-up raid, but this was cancelled by Admiral Chuichi Nagumo, commander of the Japanese carrier force, because the carriers *Lexington* (CV-2) and *Enterprise* (CV-6) were not at Pearl Harbor. ('CV' was the designator for a fleet carrier, and the aviation squadrons on each carrier were numbered accordingly.) Fortuitously, they had been dispatched to ferry Marine F4Fs and SB2U dive-bombers to Wake and Midway, respectively, though the 'Big E' was 150 miles out from Pearl to the south-west, and would surely not have survived an aerial attack had Nagumo shown more ambition. Without these two 'flat-tops', and the *Saratoga*, which had also been at sea during the attack, the Navy would have been unable to offer any immediate response to the débâcle. These carriers, plus the, *Ranger* (CV-4), *Wasp* (CV-7), *Hornet* (CV-8) (which launched sixteen B-25s against Japan on 18 April 1942) and *Yorktown* (CV-5), would form the backbone of the new Pacific Fleet commanded by Admiral Chester W. Nimitz.

Langley had become the first American carrier to

Below: Vought O2SU Kingfisher in flight. On 31 December 1941 the US Navy had on inventory fifty-two OS2U-1s, 151 OS2U-2s, and 332 OS2U-3s.
(*USN*)

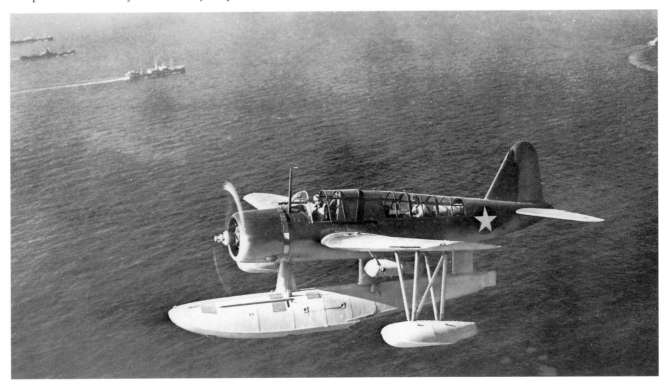

Above: Consolidated PBY-4 in flight. In 1941 PBY pilots were sent to Britain to instruct RAF Coastal Command in Catalina operations. One of them, Ensign Leonard B. Smith USN, with Pilot Officer Briggs, found the elusive German battleship *Bismarck* after the sinking of HMS *Hood*, and trailed it for four hours. In August 1941 six PBY-5s of VP-73 and six Martin PBM Mariners of VP-74 were based at Skerja Fjord in Iceland. (*Consolidated*)

be commissioned, on 20 March 1922, converted from *Jupiter*, a pre-World War One fleet collier, by adding a 534ft by 64ft wooden flight deck. The Washington Naval Treaty signed on 6 February 1921 had prohibited the Navy from adding a new class of large battlecruisers to its fleet, but it did allow two ex-battlecruisers – the *Lexington* and the *Saratoga*, both commissioned in 1927 – to be converted to aircraft carriers. Upon its introduction into fleet service in 1934, *Ranger* became the first aircraft carrier from the keel up. During September 1937–October 1941, four more flat-tops – the *Yorktown*, *Enterprise*, *Wasp* and *Hornet* – had joined the fleet and 5,260 aircraft were in service. In July 1940 eleven new carriers were authorised.

The Pacific War has always captured the headlines, but in Europe Navy flat-tops played a large role in operations against the Axis, and before America's entry into the war carrier aircraft flew neutrality patrols in the Atlantic. Three aircraft carriers, the *Wasp*, *Yorktown* and *Ranger*, together with air patrols by PBY and P2Y amphibians and Martin PBM Mariners, were active in the region. On 7 December 1941 *Wasp* was at sea with *Yorktown's* fighter squadron VF-5 aboard. In April 1942 *Wasp* arrived at Scapa Flow in the Orkneys and she transported forty-seven RAF Spitfires to Malta, delivering them on 20 April. After one more delivery, in May, the *Wasp* returned to America for deployment to the Pacific. She was sunk by Japanese torpedoes off Guadalcanal on 15 September 1942 with the loss of 200 men and forty-six aircraft.

Above: N3N in the famous 'Yellow Peril' scheme. With the Naval Expansion Act of June 1940, even more pilots were needed and hundreds of additional primary trainers had to be found for them. Initial orders were placed with the Naval Aircraft Factory in Philadelphia, PA, for 500 N3N-3s, but more landplane trainers were needed. (*Author*)

Below: Aloft in an N2S-3 Navy trainer, the most numerous of all Navy Stearmans used for primary training. In 1939 the USN had reassessed its expanded pilot training needs and how best to meet them. No longer would all pilots be seaplane trained. They now required convertible landplane/seaplane primary training airplanes. About half of all USN pilots were primary trained on the N2S-1 to -5 series of Stearmans, and eventually N2S production reached 3,785. (*Author*)

Ranger also delivered American-built fighters to the Gold Coast in Africa in April and June 1942. She then embarked her air group and in November 1942 took part in the Anglo-American landings in Morocco and Algeria, codenamed Operation 'Torch'. *Ranger* and the escort carrier *Suwannee* (ACV-27) operated off Casablanca, while *Sangamon* (ACV-26) and *Santee* (ACV-29) operated in the northern and southern areas respectively. (On 15 July 1943 escort carriers were redesignated CVE.) Altogether, the carriers contributed a combined strength of sixty-two Douglas SBD-3 Dauntlesses and Grumman TBF-1 Avengers, and 109 F4F Wildcats. On 3 October 1943 *Ranger*'s SBD-3s and Avengers of VB-4 and VT-4, and her Wildcats, took part in 'Leader', the Royal Navy operation against Axis shipping in and around Bodo harbour on the Norwegian coast. A year later, in August 1944, two escort carriers, *Tulagi* (CVE-72) and *Kasaan Bay* (CVE-69), each equipped with a squadron of twenty-four F6F-5 Hellcats, were prominent in Operation 'Anvil/Dragoon', the invasion of southern France. For the remainder of the war the CVEs fought the German U-boats in Atlantic waters.

Meanwhile, in the Pacific, by mid-April 1942 the Japanese were well on the way to total domination in the New Guinea–New Britain–Solomon Islands area of the South Pacific. Fleet Admiral Isoroku Yamamoto, the Japanese Commander-in-Chief, had predicted that Japan could win a series of rapid victories with the naval strength at their disposal, but he knew that in the long term Japan's industrial capacity would prove insufficient against that of America and her allies. They had been powerless to stop the capture of the Philippines, East Indies, Guam and Wake, but at sea it would be a different story. Within a six-month period of 1942, four naval battles involving the USN and the Imperial Japanese Navy took place, and their outcome affected the whole course of the war. Of the twenty naval battles between the two navies in the last three years of the war, five would be fought between aircraft carriers.

The first was the Battle of the Coral Sea, 7–8 May 1942, when the Japanese sent a seaborne task force to take Tulagi in the Solomons and Port Moresby in New Guinea, which Japan needed to establish a base for the invasion of Australia itself. Nimitz dispatched Task Force 17, under the command of Rear-Admiral Frank J. Fletcher, to try to forestall the intended

Below: Training for war. Cadets cut their teeth at NAS Pensacola on BT-Stearman and N3Ns. Navy aviation training offered the 'finest aviation training in the world', to quote from the NAS Pensacola edition of *Wing Tips*. It went on to say, 'From this training, and through his associations with the Naval Service, the successful Aviation Cadet emerges as a designated Naval Aviator with outstanding qualifications for service either in the Navy or in civil life. He is assured that desirable standing and prestige in his profession which is the aim and recompense of the ambitious young American.' (*Author Coll.*)

Above: Ordnancemen disarm VF-6's F4F-3As clustered on the deck of the USS *Enterprise* following the raid on Marcus Island, 4 March 1942. The Wildcat was to prove one of the outstanding fleet fighters of World War Two and the Navy's standard single-seat carrier-borne fighter, 1941–3. Fighter squadrons aboard US carriers were equipped with the F4F-3 Wildcat to provide cover for the scout, bomber and torpedo squadrons aboard. The rudder strips applied to the tails of the Wildcats, and the red centres in the white stars, were both discontinued on 15 May 1942.

(*Grumman*)

Above: In April and June 1942 the *Ranger* delivered USAAF Curtiss P-40 Warhawks to the Gold Coast of Africa, then embarked her air group. In November, she took part in the Anglo-American landings (Operation 'Torch') against Vichy French forces in Morocco and

Algeria. *Ranger*, seen here launching an F4F-4 Wildcat of VF-9 from the flight deck, with a tie-down rope still dangling from the port bomb rack, operated off Casablanca with the escort carrier USS *Suwannee* (ACV-27). (*Grumman*)

Japanese invasion forces. TF17 consisted of seven cruisers, a screen of destroyers and the carriers *Yorktown*, Fletcher's flagship, and *Lexington*, commanded by Rear-Admiral Aubrey W. Fitch. *Yorktown*'s air group consisted of Devastators of VT-5 (Torpedo), Dauntless dive-bombers of VS-5 (Scout) and VB-5 (Bomber), and F4F-3 Wildcat fighters of VF-42, while *Lexington* had embarked Devastators of VT-2, Dauntless dive-bombers of VS-2 and VB-2, and F4F-3 Wildcat fighters of VF-2.

On 7 May ninety-three aircraft from *Lexington* and *Yorktown* attacked the light carrier *Shoho*, which sank at 1135 hours. Next day, American aircraft located the *Shokaku* and the *Zuikaku*, and the Japanese located the *Lexington* and *Yorktown*. The 'Lady Lex' was hit by a torpedo and later exploded and sank after it had been abandoned. The Battle of the Coral Sea was unique in that it was the first sea battle in which the opposing ships neither engaged nor even saw each other. At the final count, the Japanese had lost eighty aircraft and approximately 900 men, while the Americans had lost sixty-six aircraft and 543 men. Coral Sea was a tactical victory for the Japanese, but strategically, American sea power had

triumphed. Not only had Japan been forced to cancel the amphibious invasion of Port Moresby in favour of a much more difficult overland campaign, but damage to the *Shokaku* and the *Zuikaku* and their air groups meant that both were unable to take part in the Battle of Midway, an island 1,300 miles north-west of Oahu, a month later.

Although the *Zuikaku* and the *Shokaku* could not be repaired in time to join the invasion fleet heading for Midway, the Japanese naval forces were formidable. To meet this threat the Americans had three carriers: the *Hornet*, the *Enterprise* (Task Force 16), and the *Yorktown* (TF17), on which repair crews at Pearl Harbor had performed miracles to get the badly damaged veteran of the Coral Sea seaworthy again. Her air group was a combination of her own and the survivors from the late lamented *Lexington*.

On 4 June battle commenced between the two American task forces and Admiral Nagumo's 1 Carrier Striking Force consisting of the *Akagi*, *Kaga*, *Hiryu* and *Soryu* covering the invasion force. Lt-Cdr Clarence W. McClusky, Air Group Commander aboard the *Enterprise*, led thirty-three SBD Dauntless dive-bombers from VB-6 and VS-6 in a search for the

Above: When America entered the war carrier squadrons normally operated three types of aircraft. Fighter squadrons flew the stubby Grumman F4F-3 Wildcat, while scout and bomber units operated the Douglas SBD-2 Dauntless dive-bomber, and torpedo squadrons flew the Douglas TBD-1 Devastator. At the time of Pearl Harbor the Dauntless was considered obsolescent, but the prolonged development of its intended successor, the Curtiss SB2C, which did not finally enter service until the end of 1943, saw the Douglas aircraft enjoy a long and successful career which was unsurpassed by any other dive-bomber in the world. During Operation 'Torch', November 1942, US carriers contributed sixty-two SBD-3s to the operation. On 3 October 1943 *Ranger*'s Dauntlesses of VB-4 (and Avengers of VT-4, and her Wildcats) took part in 'Leader', the Royal Navy operation against Axis shipping in and around Bodo harbour on the Norwegian coast. (*Douglas*)

enemy fleet. The rest of the air groups aboard the *Enterprise* and *Hornet* followed at intervals, but even using double launching methods, getting the large formations airborne took about an hour to complete. The time lag between formation take-offs and a build-up of layers of broken cloud en route scattered the formation and ruled out effective fighter protection for the slow-flying TBD-1 Devastators. The *Enterprise*'s fourteen TBDs in VT-6, led by Lt-Cdr Eugene E. Lindsey, flew on to their targets alone, while the ten Wildcats in VF-6, commanded by Lt James S. Gray, followed, thirty-six F4F-3s remaining behind to take it in turns to patrol over the task force.

The *Hornet*'s ten Wildcats in VF-8, led by Lt-Cdr Samuel G. Mitchell, failed to make contact with Lt-Cdr John C. Waldron's fifteen Devastators in VT-8 and tacked on to the thirty-five Dauntlesses divided into VB-8, led by Lt-Cdr Robert R. Johnson, and VS-8, commanded by Lt-Cdr Walter F. Rodee, leaving Waldron's torpedo-bombers to fly on alone. In the time since take-off from the American carriers Nagumo's Task Force had changed course to the north-east. The four air groups therefore arrived at the anticipated position and found no carriers. The *Hornet*'s dive-bombers decided to search south, but finding nothing and getting low on fuel, many of the Dauntlesses were forced to land back on *Hornet* or refuel at Midway. Unfortunately, the Wildcats burned up fuel far quicker and all ten in VF-8 were forced to ditch in the sea. Upwards of fifty Zeros attacked the Devastators in VT-8 and shot down all fifteen aircraft.

The fourteen TBDs in VT-6 from *Enterprise*, which singled out the *Kaga*, and *Yorktown*'s air group consisting of twelve TBD-1s from VT-3 and six F3F-3s of VF-3 led by Lt-Cdr John S. Thatch, and seventeen Dauntlesses from VS-3 and VB-3, which proceeded to attack the *Soryu*, were also overwhelmed. Zeros shot down eleven of the TBD-1s in VT-6, and ten of VT-3. Although none of the TBD-1s' torpedoes found their mark, Dauntlesses from the *Enterprise* arrived overhead unseen and scored hits on the *Akagi* and the *Kaga*, while Dauntlesses from the *Hornet* scored three hits on the *Soryu*. Within the space of five minutes the dive-bombers had crippled all three carriers. Eleven of the SBDs from the *Enterprise* were forced to ditch after running out of fuel on the return flight to the carrier. A force of bombers from the *Hiryu* discovered and damaged the *Yorktown*, which was crippled in a second strike by torpedo-bombers and had to be abandoned.

She was sunk on 7 June by two torpedoes from a Japanese submarine after being taken in tow. Finally, the *Hiryu* was located by forty Dauntlesses from *Enterprise* and *Hornet*, who scored four hits and crippled the Japanese carrier. *Hiryu* was finally abandoned on the morning of the 5th before being sunk by Japanese torpedoes.

The Battle of Midway proved to be the decisive turning point in the Pacific War. Although Japanese fighters had scored an impressive victory over the American aviation units, which lost eighty-five out of 195 aircraft, a large part of the élite in Japanese naval aviation had also perished. The loss of four of her carriers meant Japan would never again dictate events in the Pacific.

Below: F4F-4 of VF-29 is moved into position on the flight deck of the USS *Santee* (AVG-29) during Operation 'Torch'. Altogether, 109 Wildcats were available to cover the amphibious landings on the North African coast. (*Grumman*)

In August the USN boldly struggled for supremacy of the sea around Guadalcanal. With Japanese reinforcements and supplies cut off by the Navy, retreat became Japan's only option. Heavy losses at Guadalcanal so weakened the Japanese Navy that it could not stop the campaign to isolate the important base at Rabaul. By April 1944 Rabaul no longer posed a threat. New large Essex-class CV and CVL escort carriers, as well as amphibious landing craft, and newer, more powerful types of aircraft such as the Grumman F6F Hellcat, the Cyclone-engined FM-2 Wildcat, the Grumman TBM/TBF Avenger and the Curtiss SB2C-1C Helldiver, also arrived from late in 1943 onwards to replace the older fighter and torpedo-bomber aircraft.

Between late 1943 and mid-1944 the advance in the South Pacific, combined with a drive in the Central Pacific, breached the Japanese defensive perimeter and opened the way for the liberation of the Philippines. While General Douglas MacArthur

---

Below: An F4F of VF-6 below deck on the USS *Enterprise* is prepared for combat. Although slower than other American fighters and out-performed by the Zero in the Pacific theatre, the Wildcat would average almost seven enemy aircraft shot down to every one F4F lost. This can be attributed to its rugged construction and the skill and tactics of its pilots. One of the most memorable feats attributed to the Wildcat occurred off Rabaul on 20 February 1942. Lt-Cdr Edward H. 'Butch' O'Hare of VF-3 single-handedly saved his carrier, *Lexington*, by breaking up an attack by nine Mitsubishi G4M 'Betty' bombers and shooting down five of them in six minutes. He became one of the first American aces and was awarded the Medal of Honor. O'Hare, now commanding the 'Big E's' CVG-6, was killed on the night of 26 November 1943 when he hit the water while taking evasive action after being fired on by an Avenger.
(*Grumman*)

Above: Heraldry of heroism. Fighting Squadron 72 (VF-72) chose the Blue Burglar Wasp and added a sailor's white hat and four boxing gloves for their insignia. (*Author*)

advanced through the South Pacific along New Guinea, the US Navy began the Central Pacific campaign, capturing bases in the Gilberts and the Marshall Islands. Carrier task groups shattered Japanese bases and intercepted their naval forces. The Gilberts were attacked and occupied in November 1943, and in February 1944 the main atolls of the Marshalls were overrun. As part of the assault on Eniwetok, the most westerly of the Marshall chain, a huge two-day air strike on the Japanese Navy base at Truk in the Carolines was carried out by the aircraft carriers in Admiral Raymond Spruance's 5th Fleet. Truk capitulated and the Japanese retreated, first to Palau and finally, in March 1944, to Singapore.

Despite these defeats, Japanese naval forces in the Pacific were far from finished. Numerically, Japan possessed a much larger carrier force than the United States, and the Navy could call upon 1,700 land-based fighters if the American fleet could be lured to a suitable killing zone either in the Palaus or the Western Carolines, where they were within air striking range from bases in the Netherlands East Indies, New Guinea, the Bismarcks, the Philippines and Singapore. Some 484 aircraft were based on Tinian, Guam and Saipan in the Marianas, while a further 114 were based in the Western Caroline Islands. With such air and naval forces at their disposal the Japanese admirals believed that if they could engage the American fleet on their terms, they could win a decisive sea battle and re-establish naval supremacy in the Pacific. They never got the chance.

The Japanese hand was forced when on 15 June 1944 massive USMC and Army forces invaded the Marianas Islands. They were backed up by Task Force 58, a huge carrier strike force composed of four self-contained task groups each with its own escorts, and commanded by Vice-Admiral Marc 'Pete' A. Mitscher. There was no mistaking the Americans' vast superiority in quality and quantity, both at sea, where fifteen fast carriers lined up against nine Imperial Japanese Navy carriers, and in the air, where TF-58 could field over 400 F6F Hellcats. TG58-1 was composed of *Hornet, Yorktown, Bataan* and *Belleau Wood*, with a total of 265 aircraft; TG58-2 was made up of *Bunker Hill, Cabot, Monterey* and *Wasp*, with 242 aircraft; TG58-3 comprised the *Enterprise*, the new *Lexington* (Mitscher's flagship), *Princeton* and *San Jacinto*, with a total of 227 aircraft; TG58-4 was composed of the *Essex, Langley* and *Cowpens* (affectionately known as the 'Mighty Moo'), with 162 aircraft. The vast Japanese fleet was composed of three forces: 'A' Force was made up of three large fleet carriers, *Shokaku, Taiho* and *Zuikaku*, with a total air strength of some 430 aircraft; 'B' Force was composed of the fleet carriers *Hiyo* and *Junyo* and the light carrier *Ryuho*, which contained 135 aircraft; 'C' Force, whose three light carriers contained only eight-eight aircraft, was employed as a diversionary force for the other two groups. All the carriers in the three forces were protected by a defensive screen of destroyers, cruisers and battleships.

The first Battle of the Philippine Sea, or the 'Marianas Turkey Shoot' as it came to be called, commenced on 11 June. TF-58 began 'softening up' the Marianas with heavy gunfire while a fighter sweep by 211 Hellcats and eight Avengers was sent in to gain fighter superiority over the islands. Japanese fighters tried in vain to intercept the Hellcats over Guam but thirty were shot down and Hellcats of VF-28 from *Monterey* destroyed six Mitsubishi G4M2 'Bettys' over Tinian. By 14 June, after four days of fighting, the US Navy pilots had destroyed almost 150 Japanese aircraft. On 12 June, Saipan and Tinian were shelled heavily. Two groups remained in the area to establish total air supremacy, while that evening TG58-1 and TG58-4 sped 650 miles north to attack Chichi Jima and Iwo Jima. On 15 and 16 June Hellcats from TG58-1 and TG58-4 brought down about ten Zeros in combat and destroyed sixty aircraft on the ground.

The fierce fighting continued on the 17th and 18th, and on 19 June the battle reached its zenith. During one action Hellcats destroyed seventy aircraft for the loss of only four of their number. Lt Alexander Vraciu of VF-16 from the *Lexington* shot down six 'Judy' dive-bombers, making him the Navy's leading ace, with eighteen 'kills'. Commander David D. McCampbell of VF-15, who was to finish the war as the US Navy's top-scoring fighter pilot with thirty-four victories and the Medal of Honor, shot down four enemy aircraft in this engagement and three more in a second action on 19 June. In all, the

Above: TBD-1 of VT-6 on board the USS *Enterprise*, dropping a Mk 13 twenty-one-inch aerial torpedo from low level. Designed in 1934, the Devastator was the first all-metal monoplane carrier aircraft when it joined the fleet in 1937, and the first operational American naval aircraft to feature hydraulically operated folded wings. But by modern standards it was too slow, had a poor rate of climb and its range was limited. The Mk 13 torpedo, whose pre-war development had suffered badly because of the lack of funding and limited testing, was very unreliable. It required that runs be made at eighty-foot altitudes at no more than eighty knots (ninety-two mph), with release no further than 1,000 yards from the target. Even so, the torpedo often failed to work properly. When America went to war in the Pacific in 1942 only about a hundred TBD-1s were available, and just twenty-five took part in the Battle of the Coral Sea, 7–8 May 1942.
(*Douglas*)

Japanese lost 243 aircraft and over thirty damaged out of 373 which had been dispatched against the American fleet, while other losses reduced the number of survivors to just 102. Some fifty-eight land-based aircraft had also been shot down in the air and another fifty-two destroyed on the ground. Japan could not hope to replace the horrendous losses in pilots and crews, while American losses amounted to just twenty-three aircraft shot down and six more lost operationally. Hellcat pilots had accounted for 250 of the enemy aircraft shot down on 19 June.

Once more in battle the opposing American and Japanese fleets, sailing 400 miles apart, never faced each other or fired their massive guns at one another. Air power had again decided the outcome of a major battle at sea, and this time there would be no recovery for Japan. In four days, 23–26 October, during the Battle of Leyte Gulf, the Imperial Navy lost twenty-four warships, including all four carriers *Chiyoda*, *Chitose*, *Zuiho* and *Zuikaku*, the last survivor of the six carriers which had launched the attack on Pearl Harbor on 7 December 1941. *Zuikaku* was sunk by a combined force from VT-19 and VT-44 from the *Lexington* (CV 16) and the *Langley* (CVL 27). The USS *Princeton* (CVL 23) was lost on 24 October (a day when Commander Dave McCampbell set an Allied record by downing nine aircraft in one mission), but the Imperial Japanese Navy would never again pose a serious threat in the Pacific.

During the second battle of the Philippine Sea, 26–27 October, American carrier planes sank a light cruiser and four destroyers. During the remaining months of the war, until early August 1945, kamikaze aircraft posed the main threat to the fast carriers in the Pacific. In fact, as a result of kamikaze action, the heaviest losses in US warships in World War Two occurred in the last year of the war. The worst casualty was the *Saratoga*, which in February 1945 was hit by four suicide planes at Iwo Jima, and put out of action for the rest of the war. In the Okinawa campaign, April 1945, kamikazes were credited with more than 275 hits or near misses on US ships. When *Intrepid* was hit on 16 April with the loss of forty aircraft, she was the fifth carrier of eleven in the operation to be struck by kamikaze aircraft. On 11 May 1945 the USS *Bunker Hill* (CV-17) was hit by two kamikazes within thirty minutes.

The fast carriers flew their last missions over Japan on 15 August 1945 when word came through that Japan had surrendered unconditionally, and the attack groups were recalled. The war in the Far East was over without an air battle, but with destruction on a massive scale when an atomic bomb was dropped on Hiroshima on 6 August, and another was exploded over Nagasaki three days later. The Japanese Government surrendered five days later, on 14 August. Although they were not the instrument of final victory, it was the US Navy, and significantly her carrier strength, that had halted the run of Japanese victories and finally destroyed Japan's naval air power. Since the day of infamy, 7 December 1941, some 6,826 aircraft of the Imperial Navy had been shot down by Naval Aviation. The official surrender ceremony took place aboard the USS *Missouri* in Tokyo Bay on 2 September 1945.

Below: USS *Lexington* afire and sinking after being abandoned on 8 May 1942 during the Battle of the Coral Sea. Japanese bombers fanned out and made a low-level torpedo attack on the 'Lady Lex', as she was affectionately known, attacking both bows at once from barely a thousand yards out and at heights ranging between fifty and 200 feet. The carrier sustained two hits and water flooded the three boiler rooms. At the same time Aichi 'Vals' dive-bombed the carrier from 17,000 feet, scoring two hits. Listing heavily, the 'Lady Lex' limped away.

Returning aircrews were still able to land on board, but escaping fuel vapour built up inside and at 1247 hours, ignited by a still-running motor generator, a great internal explosion rocked the ship. A second major explosion occurred at 1445 and the fires soon got out of control. At 1710 her crew were taken aboard the *Yorktown*. At 1956 hours the destroyer *Phelps* put five torpedoes into her and the 'Lady Lex' sank beneath the waves. (*USN*)

Above: During the Battle of the Coral Sea, 7–8 May 1942, SBD Dauntlesses sank the small carrier *Shoho* and disabled the fleet carrier *Shokaku*. By the end of May 1942, VF-3, VF-6 and VF-8 had been equipped with twenty-seven F4Fs each and they took part in the Battle of Midway, 4–7 June.

During the battle, 110 SBD-3s from *Hornet*, *Enterprise* and *Yorktown* destroyed all four Japanese carriers and turned the tide of the Pacific War.
(*Grumman*)

Opposite above: Eleven of the fourteen TBD-1s of VT-6 spotted on *Enterprise* prior to take-off in the Battle of Midway, 4 June 1942. The Devastators, which had proved totally unsuitable for modern combat operations, remained aboard after Coral Sea only because there was no time to embark new Grumman TBF-1 Avengers. At Midway, Lt-

Cdr Eugene E. Lindsey led his fourteen TBD-1s of VT-6 to their targets alone, and singled out the *Kaga*, but Zeros shot down eleven of the Devastators and none of the TBD-1s' torpedoes found their mark. Of the forty-one TBD-1s that took part at Midway, only five of those launched returned.
(*Douglas*)

Opposite below: VF-6's F4F Wildcats and VT-6's SBD Dauntlesses aboard the USS *Enterprise* on 15 May 1942. At first, each squadron aboard a carrier totalled eighteen aircraft of these respective types, so a typical air group consisted of thirty-six SBDs, eighteen F4Fs and eighteen TBD-1s, or seventy-two aircraft. The American post-mortem into the Battle of the Coral Sea revealed that not enough Wildcats were embarked, so the fighter complement aboard carriers was increased from eighteen to twenty-seven. The aircraft were new-type F4F-4s which were among the first of the newer types to reach the Navy. The F4F-4, which had arrived in Hawaii just too late for service aboard *Lexington* and *Yorktown* at Coral Sea, was

produced with folding wings for greater accommodation aboard the carriers, and fitted with six machine-guns instead of four. At Coral Sea the *Yorktown*, or the 'Fighting Lady' as she was known, had been hit by an 800lb bomb dropped by an Aichi 'Val', which went right through the flight deck and exploded three decks below, killing sixty-six sailors. A fire broke out and thick black smoke poured through a hole in the deck, but she remained afloat. *Yorktown* made it to Pearl Harbor where, incredibly, the carrier was patched up and ready for sea again after just three days, in time to take part in the Battle of Midway.
(*Grumman*)

Below: Pilots of VT-8 inspecting one of the first TBF-1 torpedo-bombers delivered to the USN in January–February 1942. The Avenger was the first single-engined US aircraft to mount a power-operated turret, and the first to carry a twenty-two-inch torpedo. Although no carrier-borne TBF-1 took part in the Battle of Midway, six Avengers from a detachment of twenty-one aircraft in VT-8 commanded by Lt Langdon K. Feiberling, which had been sent to Hawaii and were based on Midway with AAC B-26s, located the Japanese fleet and made low-level attacks. Seventeen Zeros already on patrol dived on the torpedo-bombers from upwards of 3,000 feet but failed to prevent the torpedoes from being launched. As they turned away after launching, the unprotected formation were easy prey for the Japanese fighters, which destroyed seven aircraft and badly damaged three others. Only one Avenger, piloted by Ensign Albert K. Earnest, with dead turret gunner AMM3c J. D. Manning and wounded radioman/tunnel gunner RM3c H. H. Ferrier aboard, and two B-26s survived to crash-land back on Midway. All the torpedoes missed their targets. On 1 February 1943 the national marking was removed from the upper right and lower left of the wings of US aircraft. (*Grumman*)

Above: George H. Gay (left), who gained immortality as the sole survivor of VT-8 in the Battle of Midway. A native of Waco, Texas, George entered the USN in February 1941 as an aviation cadet. Throughout his training he flew N3Ns and N2Ss and progressed to F2Fs, F3Fs, SBCs and SBNs. Gay was commissioned 6 September 1941, and ordered to advanced carrier training, NAS Norfolk, Virginia. He reported to VT-8 on 2 November 1941. The squadron was commanded by Lt-Cdr John Charles

Waldron, a man who was to make an indelible impression on George's life. Ensign Gay had been at Norfolk only thirty days when the Japanese attacked Pearl Harbor. VT-8 was assigned to the carrier *Hornet* and went aboard early in March 1942. *Hornet* proceeded via convoy through the Panama Canal and on up the west coast to Alameda NAS, where it took aboard Jimmy Doolittle's AAF B-25s to the far western Pacific. On 17 April 1942, the *Hornet* launched the Doolittle raiders towards Japan. Six weeks later Admiral Chester W. Nimitz's fleet engaged the vastly superior (in numbers) Japanese naval sea and air forces at Midway. VT-8 lost every one of its fifteen TBDs and all of the aircrewmen, except one – Ensign Gay, who piloted the last plane in the formation. He heeded the words of John Waldron, who before the raid had urged, 'I want each of us to do his utmost to destroy our enemies. If there is only one plane left to make a final run-in, I want that man to go in and get a hit.' Despite the loss of his gunner and wounds to his arm and leg, Gay managed to get his torpedo away before he skimmed over the bow of the carrier and crashed into the sea. He miraculously emerged as his aircraft began to sink with his dead gunner aboard. Luckily, his rubber seat cushion floated clear and Gay grabbed it. He bobbed in the sea, clutching his seat, until dusk, when he finally inflated his dinghy without fear of being strafed by Zeros. Gay was picked up by a Catalina the following day. He had been in the water for thirty hours. George Gay recovered from his wounds in a Navy hospital at Pearl Harbor and he flew throughout the rest of the war. Post-war he joined TWA and flew for the airline for thirty years. Gay died in Kennestone Hospital, Marietta, GA, on 21 October 1994. (*Author*)

Below: The Grumman F6F, which had first flown in prototype shortly after the Battle of Midway on 26 June 1942, became the Navy's standard fast carrier fighter. The Hellcat made its combat debut on 31 August 1943, flown by VF-9 on *Essex* and VF-5 on *Yorktown* on strikes against Marcus Island. It was faster in level flight and the dive than the Mitsubishi A6M5 Zero. (*Grumman*)

Below: On 4 June *Yorktown* fell victim to an assault by eighteen Aichi D3A 'Vals' from the *Hiryu*. *Yorktown*'s Wildcats intercepted the bombers and shot down seven 'Vals' and four Zeros, but one bomb hit the flight-deck and the explosion started a fire in the hangar below. A second bomb caused extensive damage to the ship's insides and knocked out most of the boilers so that the carrier's speed was severely reduced and then finally halted. A third bomb, which penetrated to the fourth deck, caused a serious fire which threatened to engulf the forward petrol tanks and ammunition stores. Despite all this, the crew managed to dampen down the raging fires and soon the ship was underway again. The Wildcats were refuelled and rearmed aboard *Enterprise* and were almost ready when a second wave of ten Nakajima 'Kate' torpedo-bombers and six Zeros appeared on radar forty miles distant. Ten F4Fs screamed into the attack, trying to get at the 'Kates', but they were fended off by the Zeros. Four Wildcats and three Zeros were shot down. The 'Kates' flew ruggedly on despite the curtain of withering fire put up by the cruisers and the gunners aboard the *Yorktown*, and attacked the carrier from four angles. Five 'Kates' were shot down but four torpedoes, launched from only 500 yards, scored two hits below the waterline. The 'Fighting Lady's' fuel tanks were sliced open and the lower decks flooded. She began listing badly and the order was given to abandon ship.
(*USN*)

Above: Despite their poor beginning, Avengers proved very successful. Aboard three carriers that began the Guadalcanal operation on 7 August 1942 they helped sink the carrier *Ryujo*, battleship *Hiei*, and the cruiser *Kinugasu*. Every new fast carrier that joined the fleet from 1943 onwards had its TBF/TBM Avenger squadron, and the torpedo-bombers took part in every major battle. Working with dive-bombers, they destroyed both of the world's largest battleships, the *Musashi* on 24 October 1944, with nineteen torpedoes (and seventeen bombs), and the *Yamato*. In the Atlantic Avengers served on escort carriers, first in support of the 'Torch' invasion, and then with anti-submarine groups. They sank their first German submarine, U-569, on 22 May 1943. Avengers on ten escort carriers shared in the sinking of forty-nine *unterseeboote* by the hunter carrier/destroyer groups. (*Grumman*)

Above: On board the USS *Saratoga* (CV-3) at dawn in November 1943 for the strike against Rabaul. (*US Navy*)

Above: The Corsair's Carrier Qualification trials (CarQuals) on board *Sangamon* in September 1942 revealed poor stalling characteristics caused by the high power and torque of the propeller, and other operating drawbacks, not least a tendency to bounce dangerously on landing (which could manifest itself later in the hands of inexperienced pilots) and a pilot visibility problem caused by the F4U's long nose ahead of the far-aft cockpit, which made it difficult for pilots to see the landing signal officer (LSO). All of these problems were later solved or alleviated, but the first US F4Us were used as land-based fighters with the USMC. The Fleet Air Arm, meanwhile, was the first to use them on carriers, on 3 April 1944. (*Tom Smith*)

Above: A formation of F4U-1s of VF-17, the first Navy squadron to see action with Corsairs when, on 11 November 1943, VF-17 landed its land-based Corsairs aboard *Bunker Hill* and *Independence* to refuel and rearm during strikes on Rabaul. The XF4U-1 flew for the first time on 29 May 1940, and when the production model appeared in June 1942, it was the first Navy fighter to exceed 400 mph in level flight. Inverted gull wings represented an unorthodox design, but its greatest attribute was its excellent overall performance which was achieved by simply designing the smallest possible airframe around the most powerful engine. (*USN via Mike Bailey*)

Above: F4U-1 flown by Lt Ira C. 'Ike' Kepford of VF-17, the leading 'Jolly Rogers' ace, with sixteen kills, in flight near Bougainville, Solomon Islands, March 1944. Late in 1944, when more fighters were needed to combat the Japanese kamikaze threat, Corsairs were at last put aboard carriers in strength, although the USMC was the first US service to operate Corsairs from a carrier, on 28 December 1944. Improvements made to the cockpit included raising the pilot's seat seven inches and fitting a larger, one-piece canopy, while pilots perfected a new landing approach, often with their port wing slightly down so that the LSO could be kept in sight. The rebound characteristics were eliminated by a modification to the main landing gear oleos, and in April 1944 any lingering doubts were removed when VF-301 used modified Corsairs to complete over one hundred successful landings in trials on board *Gambier Bay*. The Corsair possessed greater speed, rate of climb and manoeuvrability than the F6F and went on to become, by far, the finest carrier-borne fighter of the war. (*USN via Mike Bailey*)

Above: Goodyear-built FG-1D BuNo88297 (G-FGID) of the Fighter Collection on finals at Duxford. This Corsair flew with the USN in 1945 and saw combat in the Marianas Islands on board the USS *Aatu*. It is painted in the livery of the Vought F4U-1A flown by Lt Ira C. 'Ike' Kepford of VF-17 'Jolly Rogers', and carries his personal markings, including sixteen miniature 'Rising Sun' emblems representing this ace's sixteen confirmed Japanese victories. The Corsair, or 'Whistling Death' as the Japanese called it, flew 64,051 sorties and destroyed 2,140 aircraft for the loss of 768 of its number (only 189 to air combat), a 11:1 ratio of kills to losses. By the time the war finished Vought had turned out 7,298 Corsairs, and Goodyear 3,941. (*Author*)

Below: A pair of SBD-5 Dauntlesses of VB-10 with arrester hooks down prepare to land on the deck of the USS *Enterprise* following a patrol during the Palau raids, 29–30 March 1944. Both aircraft carry Yagi radar antenna beneath the wings. (*USN*)

Below: The Avenger was the first American aircraft to be fitted with forward-firing High Velocity Aerial Rockets (HVARs), six being launched from three 'zero-length' rails beneath each side of the wing. They were first used in action against a U-boat on 11 January 1944. Originally, HVARs were fitted with 3.5-inch ogive warheads, but in 1944 five-inch rockets became available. A full weapons load of six gave the aircraft a weight of fire equivalent to a destroyer's broadside. The USMC began land-based operations with Avengers at Guadalcanal in November 1942, and eight Marine Corps squadrons used them in combat in the Pacific, or on escort carriers, by 1945. Post-war, Avengers, like this one, continued to serve aboard fleet carriers. (*Roland H. Baker*)

Above: Curtiss SB2C-1C Helldivers prepare to take off from the flight deck of the USS *Bunker Hill* in June 1944. The SB2C-1C was designed to replace the SBD-5 Dauntless, but required more maintenance than the Dauntless and carried only the same bomb load with no improvement in range. Crews dubbed the Helldiver the 'Son-of-a-bitch, second class'. Plans were considered for re-equipping with SBDs again in July 1944, but Helldivers soldiered on until the war's end. (*USN*)

Above: On 20 June 1944, during the last day of the first Battle of the Philippine Sea, Avengers from the *Enterprise* sighted the Japanese fleet 300 miles from the American carriers, and radioed its position to Admiral Mitscher. If Mitscher sent off his aircraft immediately they could reach the seven remaining Japanese carriers, but it meant they would have to land back on their carriers in the dark. He pondered for a brief moment, then turned to his staff on the bridge of the *Lexington* and said, 'Launch 'em.' At about 1630, fifty Helldivers, twenty-seven Dauntlesses and fifty-four Avengers, escorted by eighty-five Hellcats, took off and headed westwards in gathering darkness. Half a dozen fuel tankers were spotted first and a section of Dauntlesses from *Wasp* broke away to attack and sink two of them. The rest of the force pressed on until thirty miles ahead it sighted the Japanese fleet protected only by about forty Zero fighters. They shot down six Hellcats, four Avengers and ten Helldivers, but only about fifteen Zeros survived the twenty-minute air battle. Four TBMs of VT-24 from *Belleau Wood*, led by Lt(jg) George B. Brown, made runs on the *Hiyo* and two hits were thought to have been made. Brown's aircraft was so badly shot up during the low-level strike that he ordered the crew to bale out. Brown stayed with his aircraft and a wingmate tried in vain to lead him back to his carrier. Brown was last seen disappearing into cloud. The Avengers and the dive-bombers caused several fires on board the *Zuikaku*. The carrier *Chiyodan* was also ablaze and a cruiser and a battleship had also been damaged. (*Grumman*)

Above: Few of the American pilots had ever made a night landing on a carrier before, and hitting the rolling decks in the darkness would be well nigh impossible. Mitscher threw caution to the wind and ordered all available lights on the carriers to be turned on to help guide the tired and over-anxious fighter and bomber pilots in. Low on fuel, they had but one chance to find the deck and land safely. Unfortunately, the assistance of searchlights, navigation lights and flightdeck floodlights and red masthead lights were not enough, and eighty aircraft either crashed on the decks or splashed into the sea. The thirsty Helldivers suffered particularly badly, and over twenty-five had to be ditched because of fuel starvation. Rescue services worked around the clock and managed to save the majority of pilots and crew. Only five SB2Cs landed back on board the carriers. Overall, only forty-nine of the 209 aircrew were lost. The Battle of the Philippine Sea, as it was officially called, ended in victory for the US Pacific Fleet. (*Author*)

Below: The 13,000-ton heavy cruiser *Nachi* under attack in Manila Bay on 5 November 1944. Avengers, and SB2C-1C Helldiver dive-bombers, scored numerous hits, causing the Myoko-class ship to sink stern-first. (*Grumman*)

Above: After the second battle of the Philippine Sea, 26–27 October 1944, the biggest threat posed to the fast carriers in the Pacific during the remaining months of the war was from kamikaze aircraft piloted by suicide pilots. In this photo, taken during the Philippines campaign, a twin-engined kamikaze aircraft narrowly misses an American carrier from CVE-71. The kamikazes' biggest victim was the USS *Saratoga*, which in February 1945 was hit by four suicide planes at Iwo Jima, and put out of action for the rest of the war.
(*Grumman*)

Below: Shades of the 'Doolittle Raiders'. A PBJ-1H Mitchell is prepared for launching during carrier trial landings and take-offs aboard the USS *Shangri-La* in November 1944. A special tail hook was fitted to the aft fuselage of the Mitchell.
(*USN via Mike Bailey*)

CHAPTER 2
HELLCAT DAWN PATROL:
Reminiscences of Carrier Duty in the Pacific, Evan Adams (VF-23)

Fighter pilots live on adrenalin. Waiting hours between flights are sustained by the subtle stream that keeps senses constantly alert. But when the time for a scramble from the deck of an aircraft carrier like the *Langley* (CVL 27) comes, the adrenalin boost rushes to a razor-sharp high, and brings all senses to a primal alert. Senses and basic reflexes become acute. The body is ready to fly.

One of the effects of the razor-edged readiness that comes with this charge of energy is that the fighter pilot passes through a reality barrier that alters the experience of flying. The aircraft becomes your body, your mind, your arms and legs. There is no sense of being a man in a machine. You are not flying an airplane, *you* are now flying through space. The horsepower, metal and man, all become one.

Somehow a transformation occurs so that one passes from performing mechanical functions to the sheer existence of flying. Every move of the aircraft is experienced as though it were oneself rolling through space. This is the exhilaration of high-speed, high-risk flying that is unique to the life of a fighter pilot who has become addicted to the risk, and the freedom of unlimited space.

In high-speed encounters that require split-second

Below: While some members of the crew of the USS *Yorktown* (CV-10) work on Cdr Charlie Crommelin's VF-5's Hellcats for the next day's air operations, other members in the background watch a Hollywood movie in one of the carrier's large hangar bays. (*Grumman*)

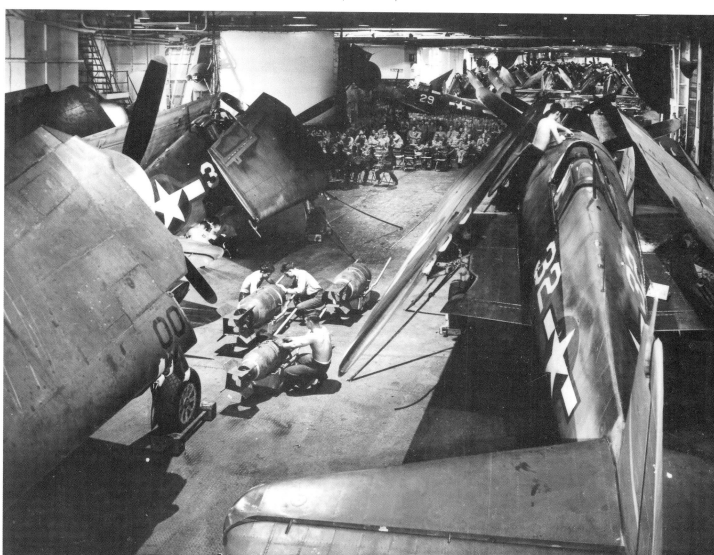

timing for reaction and survival, only space and existence remain; the sense of time disappears. This is the altered state of consciousness that comes in encounters that mean 'kill or be killed'. The roar of the 2,000hp radial engine disappears from the conscious experience of sound. There is no up or down, only flight. The familiar reference points of horizon, earth and sky are known intuitively but not seen.

The transition from earthling to flying being is a process. A short time ago you were groping your way across the pitching deck of the *Langley* towards the dim outline of a Hellcat barely visible in the pre-dawn black. The cold ocean air blowing across the deck chills you into a new level of wakefulness. The acrid fumes of diesel whipping from the ship's stacks burn your nostrils as the carrier is picking up speed to get wind across the deck for launch. Lethal blades twisting on 2,000 horsepower slash through the gusts of wind and fumes as the pilots, plane

captains and deck-handlers crawl through the last darkness of night to find cockpits, chocks and shoulder harness.

The carrier deck is an arena of controlled tension. Plane captains stand on the wing root to buckle in the pilot. Everyone knows what to do, and no one is speaking. The noise makes conversation impossible. Life has been reduced to reflex action and hand gestures. The catapult is already groaning into the rear-cocked position, ready to hurl the first fighter into the darkness. And a Hellcat creeps forward on the pitching deck in obedience to two dim yellow wands waving a silent language through the darkness to the pilot.

Everything is now dependent on inches of space, clear signals, total trust, and wind across the deck. The mind rushes through a maze of survival checks. Your hands retouch every vital adjustment: fuel mix, blade pitch, trim-tabs, throttle crimp, seat lock, shoulder harness bind. Your eyes are fixed on the

Above: F6F-3 of VF-16 is launched from the flight deck of the new *Lexington* (CV-16) in the waters between Makin in the Gilbert Islands and Mili in the Marshalls on 23 November 1943, during the invasion of the Gilberts. *Yorktown* can be seen in the background with VF-5's Hellcats embarked after recovery from an earlier strike. (*Grumman*)

Above: Lt-Cdr Paul D. Buie, CO, VF-16, exults with his 'Pistol Packin' Airedales' aboard the *Lexington*. Near Makin Island on 23 November 1943 Buie led twelve Hellcats against twenty-one Zekes, and in one pass they shot down seventeen and claimed four 'probables'. Buie downed two of the enemy, while Ensign Ralph Hanks, in his first combat, scored five confirmed victories and one 'probable' to become the first Hellcat pilot to achieve ace status and the first to become an 'ace in a day'. Next day, VF-16 claimed another thirteen confirmed and six probables. Buie's own score for World War Two was nine victories. (*Grumman*)

yellow wands, and you don't see anything else. Toes are alert to respond to the commands of the directing wands. Engine temperature, manifold pressure, oil pressure, artificial horizon, all are seen at once, without looking.

The wands stand upright and still. You are on the catapult. Some deck-mule has crawled on his belly to lock your tail into the holding-ring. Another deck-mule has hooked you into the catapult cable that will act as your sling-shot. Your eyes belong only to two pale yellow wands. You are about to be flung into space, and it's all intense concentration now. It's also very dark.

One wand begins whirling through the darkness. You pour on total throttle and lock it into place with a quick twist of the binding clamp. Your eyes never leave the whirling wand, it's the last signal before life or death. Your future hangs on the motion of the wands, catapult steam pressure, and reflexes. With your head back against the collision pad, your left hand comes up from the throttle quadrant, across your chest, and touches your right shoulder. Hisses

. . . boom . . . inertia forces your body against the metal bucket seat, your head pinned into the collision pad by brute thrust. In seconds, engine, fuselage, wings and pilot disappear into the darkness at 100 mph.

Ten minutes ago you were just a tense pilot in the ready room making final marks on your navigation chart to identify 'point option' – where you hope the carrier will be three hours from now. The aroma of black coffee is the only thing in your senses right now. Secret codes for the day were penciled into your knee pad. Standby pilots sit on the edge of their seats. Will all planes get off? From first movement along the dark deck that began with the wave of the magic wands until the hiss . . . boom . . . thrust took 160 seconds. And now the carrier has disappeared in the darkness behind you. You are flying. And the solid deck and the world have disappeared in the night.

But you must now grope for the plane that flashed off the catapult one minute before you. Somewhere out there in the last cover of night another Hellcat is beginning a slow climbing turn, shortening the arc for a closing rendezvous for the following Hellcats that are sneaking into position by visual braille. You bank slowly to the port with your eyes fixed on the darkness ahead. Your hands have already instinctively pulled up landing gear, slowly lifted flaps, adjusted trim tabs, prop pitch and fuel mix. The real world has disappeared in the black of night. Suddenly, you realise that you are cold, but there is no time to feel anything.

You are searching for a blue pin-point of flame, blazing from the exhaust stack of a 2,000 horsepower Pratt & Whitney radial somewhere out there in the pre-dawn dark. You finally spot the blue flame ahead. Now you begin tightening your turn to creep into position under another wing. The blue flame has replaced the yellow wands as your reference point for survival. Every move is now made like a tense airborne ballet, dancing in reflex rhythm to the blue flame that tells you where you are in relation to another set of wings nearby. You hear the roar of your engine only distantly, as if from another place. Listening to the engine is intuitive, like listening for your heart beat.

Four Hellcats have found each other in the pre-dawn darkness through instinct and the primal

---

Below: F6F-3 Hellcat of Air Group Two's VF-8 'Fighting 8' is manhandled into position for take-off from the Essex-class carrier USS *Bunker Hill* (CV-17), 12 October 1944. (*Grumman*)

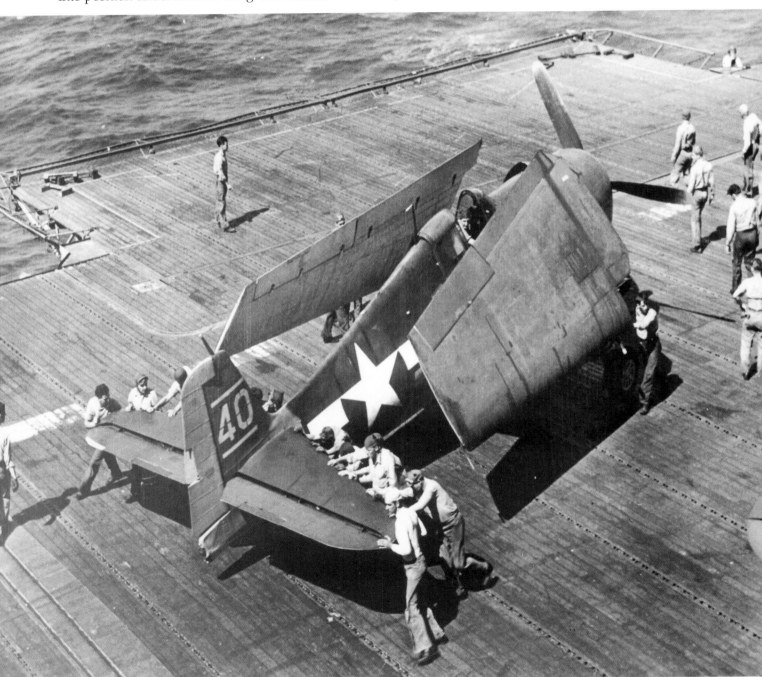

Above: Restored F6F-5K BuNo80141 showing the famous 'Felix the Cat' emblem of Fighting Squadron Six and the Japanese flag victory symbols which represent nine of Vraciu's victories gained flying F6F-5K BuNo40467 with VF-6 (See page 40). The fuselage of this aircraft survived scrapping after the war ended and has been married to the wings and tail of F6F-5K BuNo80141, and the centre section of BuNo08831, for restoration to airworthy condition. 80141 now forms part of the Fighter Collection at Duxford. (*Author*)

search through black space, more like airborne braille where the eyes have replaced the fingers in the discovery. The eyes have taken on their night vision duty through peripheral awareness. Slowly the adrenalin subsides to a maintenance level. Time suddenly comes back into existence and you are conscious that you are flying through both time and space. If all goes well you hope to find 'point option' and a clear deck three hours later. By then the sun will be up. The energy of the 3.00 a.m. breakfast seems to have been consumed in the take-off and rendezvous in the dark. You know that below you there is nothing but ocean for a thousand miles, but you can't see it. Sky and ocean have reunited in the dark of night. This night even the moon refuses to help.

Finally, four Hellcats have blended into a tight airborne vee, seeming to be motionless, climbing at 130 knots airspeed, climbing through the night to claim the high country, to be at 20,000ft, 'on top', when dawn breaks.

You recognise the voice crackling over the VHF frequency as the division leader announces our arrival on station: 'Patriot chicks at Angels 20°.' Fuel mixture is leaned out to minimum consumption and maximum engine efficiency for the altitude. The turbo-blower was kicked in at 11,000 feet to gulp the rarefied air. And now prop pitch is set for paddling along in the thin quiet of higher altitude. It's very cold, and your jump suit is still wet with the sweat of your adrenalin boost.

The fighter director breaks into the low static of the VHF frequency from his position deep inside the Combat Information Centre back at the ship. 'Make your roosters crow!' he commands. Obediently, we trigger the switch that flashes a radar signal back to the ship that identifies us as 'friendlies', and he knows he has located our blip on his radar scope. We are now on station.

Left: Commander David McCampbell, Commander Air Group 15, USS *Essex* (CV-9), pictured in F6F-5 BuNo70143 *Minsi III* (Minsi was a nickname for his girlfriend, Miss Mary Blatz). On 24 October 1944, the opening day of Battle of Leyte Gulf (also called the second battle of the Philippine Sea, and the same day that the *Princeton* (CVL-23) was lost), McCampbell, assisted by just one other Hellcat, intercepted and daringly attacked a formation of sixty fighters, shooting down nine of them, completely disorganising the enemy group and forcing the remainder to abandon their attack on the task force before a single aircraft could reach the fleet. For this action, the destruction of another seven in one day, 19 June 1944, and his inspired leadership of Air Group 15, McCampbell was awarded the Medal of Honor. McCampbell scored twenty or more victories in *Minsi III*, which, regrettably, was lost in an accident in December 1944 when it was being flown by his replacement. Twice an ace in a day, McCampbell was the top-scoring naval pilot in World War Two, with thirty-four confirmed victories. (*USN*)

Light has begun to break in the east through the scattered clouds. The clustered Hellcats are now mutually visible. We spread out a bit, floating effortlessly in space. The oxygen mask helps clear the mind, sharpen the eyes. This is the first combat air patrol of the day, on station ready for any early-morning attack on the fleet that might sneak out from some Japanese position. Our division leader's hand signals a 'trigger action' as if he is firing a pistol over his head. It's time to spread out and test fire guns to be sure everything is operational. Firing switches for the guns are flipped to 'on' position. A brief squeeze of the trigger on the stick and a *bruummmmmp* erupts from six fifty-calibre machine-

Below: Lt(jg) Alexander Vraciu, of Romanian parentage, kneels on the wing of F6F-3 white 19/BuNo40467 of VF-6, which was assigned to him in January 1944. Flying from the *Essex*, the former wingman for 'Butch' O'Hare, CO of 'Fighting Six', destroyed two 'Betty' bombers in this Hellcat on 29 January. On 16 February, flying in this aircraft from *Intrepid*, Vraciu shot down three 'Zekes' and a 'Rufe' floatplane over Truk to take his score to nine. On this momentous day about 250 of Truk's 365 combat aircraft were either destroyed or damaged, and 124 more were claimed shot down in aerial combat. Following the torpedoing of *Intrepid* on the night of the 16th, which limped into Pearl Harbor on 24 February, 40467 was transferred to VF-18 for training new pilots, and was then retired to NATTC Chicago on 29 August 1944. Meanwhile, on 29 April Vraciu, now with VF-16 on board *Lexington*, became the Navy's fifth double ace, only the second Hellcat pilot to reach double figures, when he destroyed two Zekes over Truk to take his score to eleven. On 19 June, during the 'Marianas Turkey Shoot' at the first Battle of the Philippine Sea, Vraciu claimed six Yokosuka D4Y 'Judy' dive-bombers to take his tally to eighteen victories, making him the Navy's leading ace, with two more than Corsair pilot Lt(jg) Ira Kepford of VF-17. Awarded the Navy Cross for his gallant performance, Vraciu scored his nineteenth and final aerial victory of the war the following day, when he shot down a Zeke (and damaged another). He returned to the US for a bond-raising tour and was there reunited with 40467, which had ten victory flags added, before both took centre stage at a large fund-raising rally at Wrigley Field, near his home in east Chicago. Despite a reluctance on the part of High Command to return him to combat, Vraciu returned to the Pacific, where, on his second sortie with VF-20, he was hit by ground fire near Luzon in the Philippines. Parachuting to safety, he joined up with Filipino guerrillas and led a unit until the Japanese surrender. He finished the war as the fourth-ranking Hellcat ace.
(*USN*)

Above: Flames flare out as the fuel aboard this Hellcat, flown by Lt(jg) William G. Bailey USNR of VF-33, explodes, and the starboard wing smashes into the island of the USS *Sangamon* on 26 February 1945 after a missed wire on landing. Bailey stepped out unhurt. (*USN via Phil Jarrett*)

guns at the leading edge of the wings, jolting the Hellcat like a stiff wind. Phosphorus tracers stitch an arc through the clouds and the sky like a line sketched by an unseen hand. The beauty of the moment conceals the lethal nature of the reason for keeping guns alive.

Billows of cloud create soft canyons through which we drift, disappear, and reappear. The sun is bright now, sky is blue. War, home, and memories are far away. We are just floating in space. It all seems motionless and effortless right now. Two hours into the circling wait for a call from fighter director, adrenalin has quieted down. Now real feelings come back. The engine roars. Instruments talk, and the radio static is monotonous. Even a spam sandwich would be welcome. We pass the time playing hand signal games to break the tense routine of waiting, waiting, waiting. Radios are for business and emergencies, not for chatter.

One Hellcat drifts wide of the formation to care for personal need. The morning coffee, plus the adrenalin burn, calls for the 'relief' tube routine that will funnel the bladder pressure out into space, vaporising in the cold air rushing past the plane's belly. Then drowsiness begins to creep into the bones. Coming off the adrenalin-lag makes one get very sleepy. You notice your wing-buddy is about to doze off, so you inch up slowly and tap his wing with your wing tip. Now he is wide awake again. We

were jolted out of our sleep of the dead before three this morning by the squadron personnel officer who carries the thankless job of waking fighter pilots for pre-dawn take-off. And it's good to keep your nearest wingman awake through the last hour of combat air patrol too. We might need each other. Time replaces space in a tense, monotonous wait, wait, wait. Heads pivot back and forth as eyes scan the sky and horizon for any spots or motion in the distance.

Finally, fighter director breaks the spell, calling for his 'patriot chicks' somewhere thirty miles away from home. He's calling on our radio frequency again, sending a coded phrase that says it's our time to come home to the security of the deck. The message is a combination of coded jargon and number signals. Our replacements are already airborne at 10,000 feet, and climbing, and the deck is spotted for our landings. We're wide awake again, tightening up the four-plane vee, descending at 500 feet per minute, and homebound. Once again we are flying, no longer paddling along on a three-hour wait on station between the fleet and the invisible enemy. The blue ocean reveals white gashes some miles ahead. Through the mid-morning haze dark spots begin to look like ships. Point option is for real. Sleeplessness is gone. A safe landing will be the last act. Catching the right wire will determine the success of the day.

Above: On 29 March 1945 Lt(jg) 'Slim' Somerville, an SB2C Helldiver pilot from the *Hancock*, lost his tail after it was cut off in a mid-air collision by one of the other Helldivers returning from a bombing raid on Japan. Aviation radioman Louis F. Jakubec, his rear-seat gunner, was killed, but Somerville got out and parachuted into Kagoshima Bay. An OS2U Kingfisher seaplane from the cruiser *Astoria* rescued him from the sea while four pilots from VF-6 dog-fought with eight Zeros. Five enemy fighters were shot down and Ensign Roland H. 'Bake' Baker (far left) describes his version of their dogfight to (from left to right) division leader Lt Robert L. 'Cherry' Klingler; Lt(jg) 'Slim' Somerville; and Ensign Willis 'Willi' H. Moeller, after their return to the *Hanna* off Okinawa following the rescue. Baker was forced to make a water landing in a Hellcat alongside the destroyer *Stemble* on the way home. 'Cherry' Klingler and Louis Davis each received the Navy Cross for their actions on 29 March, while Roland Baker and Willi Moeller each received the Distinguished Flying Cross. Next day, and again on 31 March, Okinawa was again hit by all squadrons in the Fighting Squadron Six. On 6 April Baker was shot up again, over an airfield on Kikai, part of the Amami O Shima Islands, when the drop tank was set on fire. The Hellcat took a lot of punishment but made it back to the *Hancock*. In the course of flying thirty missions over Okinawa, Wake and the Japanese home islands, Baker won the DFC, the Air Medal, and the Gold Star in lieu of a second Air Medal, shooting down one Japanese plane. (*Roland H. Baker*)

We approach the task force from the coded direction of the day to confirm that we are 'friendlies'. Our 'roosters' crow to confirm our identity, and we feel safe to come into the range of the five-inch anti-aircraft guns of the protective destroyer screen. Hopefully, no trigger-happy gunners will mistake us for someone else. The task force has already turned into the prevailing wind, and the carriers are at flank speed to give maximum wind over the decks to reduce landing speeds. Wind, wave, air and skill must work together to get home.

At 200 feet upwind near our carrier we break up the wide right-hand echelon in individual peel-offs, and head downwind, fifteen seconds apart. As we come abreast of mid-ship on this last leg home, the adrenalin needed for landing slot rushes back into the head again. Wheels down, full flaps, tail hook down, prop pitch into full low, trim tabs fiddled to get the decelerating Hellcat into a comfortable trim, fuel goes back to total rich mix for maximum power recovery. Gun switches are checked to ensure that the landing will not activate the trigger and spray the deck with a hail of fifty-calibre shells. Now it's all split-second reflexes once again into a landing aboard the ship. The most precarious moment of the morning is coming fast.

Hanging the Hellcat on the prop at eighty-five knots, we make the final tight left bank into the landing slot and pick up the landing signal officer on the fantail of the carrier. Now we are visually locked on the outstretched arms with two large canvas paddles giving gentle cues to correct any variance to landing attitude. Now we're hanging on the prop at seventy-eight knots, still in a turn, approaching the fantail from astern of the carrier. The ship is coming up very fast, the carrier is rolling a lazy five degrees from side to side. The fantail rises and falls in rhythm to the wave action with fifteen-foot surges of the deck. The cockpit canopy has been rolled back and locked open so that a quick exit can be made if we find the ocean rather than the deck. A wallowing destroyer hovers alongside of the carrier as a friendly watchdog with swimmers at the deck railings ready to go after a downed pilot. It makes you feel safer. A spy-glass spotter confirming that our incoming plane has wheels and hook down for the one chance at landing stands near the landing signal officer.

We are roaring towards two possible options that will come from the paddles of the signalman. Wave-off, go around for another try, as mandatory as life and death. Or, tensely waiting for the 'cut' – the welcomed paddle-across-the-throat signal that says, 'Drop it in for a crash-landing,' you're home!

Kaaabloomm onto the deck in a nose-high stall. The 'Jesus Christ' wire is the last chance before rolling into the barrier. No chance for a go-around now.

But we catch the third wire and the Hellcat wrenches to a violent and welcome jerk. The tail hook inertia throws the plane into a reverse 5Gs, and then all stops. A deck-mule jumps from the catwalk onto the pitching deck, slides under the tail of the Hellcat like a man skidding to third base. He jerks the hook free from the wire. Ahead on the deck, a signalman whirls his hand in a fast circle above his head, saying, 'Full throttle.' The steel cable barrier drops in split-second timing, and the Hellcat leaps across to the safe side. Fifteen seconds later another Hellcat lurches onto the deck, grabbing the fourth wire in the space your Hellcat occupied just seconds before.

Taxying forward to a nesting place on deck is the last act before throttle-chop. The deck is solid and comforting. The welcome hand signal across the throat says, 'Kill it!' A couple of gulps from the faithful Pratt & Whitney and it dies quietly, while the prop demands its freedom to complete its lethal momentum. A pack of deck-mules rush up to each front wing edge, give the signal to pop the locking pins, and push each wing up into its folded resting place. The Hellcat is at home in its nesting place in the tightly packed rows of fighters and torpedo bombers.

Everything is quiet for the first time in more than three hours. No more vibration. No constant alert to the sound of the radial engine. No more instrument panel to scan. The sense of space shifts back to the awareness of time. Fatigue becomes very real. The plane captain jumps on the wing smiling to see his charge safely on the deck, and his pilot back home. He checks all switches to be sure all systems are dead.

As you walk slowly back across the deck to the catwalk ladder, headed for the pilot ready room and debriefing, the last adrenalin boost is slowly ebbing. Dropping the 'chute to the floor, and sinking into a ready room seat, you try to decelerate your mind and body. It was a very routine day. Pre-dawn take-off, blue-blaze search for the join-up in the black, climb-out, and settle into the protective circle on station waiting for the unknown.

Tomorrow morning we'll repeat the same cycle. But tomorrow may be the moment when the adrenalin pumps into a maximum charge as a flight of suicide-bent 'Judys' come onto the radar scope in the Combat Information Centre, headed for the task force, and especially the flat-tops. But for now it's time to doze in the ready room while a game of acey-deucy goes on at the back of the room. The flight surgeon hands around some half-pints of brandy to any pilot that needs a nerve tonic. The codes for the day on the chart board slowly dim out of view. Slowly the sensation of flying changes to the roll and pitch of the carrier. Someone else is now at 20,000 feet in harm's way where you were in the pre-dawn darkness a long time ago.

On 11 May 1945 the *Langley* pulled out of the battle-line, where the carrier was with Task Force 58, the Fast Carrier Groups, and the ship was ordered to Hawaii, and then to the USA, for repair and refitting etc. The *Langley* had been at sea continuously for eighteen months without a port of call, other than advanced anchorage at Ulithi Atoll. Donald White, Squadron skipper, had been shot down over Tokyo, and assumed dead. He showed up in a prisoner-of-war camp near Yokohama, Japan, in September 1945. VF-23 came back to NAS Alameda at the end of May 1945. On return to San Francisco Bay, eight airmen, the fighter pilots, were assigned to reorganise VF-23 with a contingent of twenty new pilots, to train and reshape the squadron onto F4U Corsairs. This was intended to prepare for using Okinawa, and other islands, as bases for the coming invasion of the Japanese homeland. Evan Adams spent the last few months of the war in the desert country of eastern Washington State training pilots on the F4U and fighter tactics. Consequently, he was in the States at the time of the dropping of atomic bombs on Japan.

CHAPTER 3
TASK FORCE 77: KOREA

Six small silver jet fighters bearing red stars on their stubby fuselages and swept-back wings took off from the safety of their air base at Antung in Manchuria, climbed rapidly to 30,000 feet and crossed the Yalu River into North Korea. It was 1 November 1950. The formation of F-51 Mustangs and F-80 Shooting Stars flying on the North Korean side of the river was surprised at the devastating closing speed of the Communist jets, whose pilots only failed to destroy the American aircraft through their own inexperience.

It was one of a series of setbacks UN forces had suffered since the Land of the Morning Calm had erupted in war on 25 June 1950 when the North Korean Army crossed the 38th Parallel, completely wrong-footing the ROK Army and its American advisers. From the outset the North Koreans had enjoyed total air superiority, but up until that fateful November day US commanders had no reason to fear the Communist air threat because only piston-engined aircraft had confronted them. Intervention by China and the appearance of the Soviet-built jets

Below: 'Start your engines.' F8F Bearcats of VF-71 onboard the USS *Leyte c.* 1949. The Bearcat was designed to replace the F6F and operate from even the smallest of carriers to help combat the Japanese kamikaze aircraft in the Pacific War. However, it only began replacing the Hellcat in fleet

service in May 1945, when F8F-1s were embarked aboard the light carrier *Langley* with VF-19, but the war ended before combat deployment in the Pacific, by which time only 151 examples had been built. (*Captain Armistead Smith*)

Left: An F8F leaving the back of the *Leyte*. Bearcats were seldom catapulted. Deck runs were less time-consuming. Many, like Captain Armistead Smith, CO of VF-71 and a World War Two Hellcat ace with eleven victories, considered the F8F to be the best of all the propeller-driven fighters. 'I found it easy to fly, fairly forgiving of mistakes, a good gunnery platform, and really an airplane to love. It made the F6F feel like a "slug".' Although the Bearcat equipped up to twenty-eight Navy squadrons 1945–9, none served in the Korean conflict because it lacked the F4U Corsair's weapons load-carrying capability and the jet's performance, despite a top speed of 447mph at 28,000 feet. (*Captain Armistead Smith*)

in North Korean airspace dramatically changed the balance of air power at a stroke.

USAF aircraft were ill suited to operate in a close air support and interdiction campaign in Korea. They needed paved runways 6,000 feet long, and these only existed in Japan, which meant that air operations over Korea were restricted to only a few minutes. Of paramount importance, therefore, was a dire need for US carriers. Flying from flat-tops Navy and Marine units could operate in the Sea of Japan and be sent off from their carriers from about seventy miles from the coast of Korea (the shallow sea bed off the east coast of Korea prevented them from getting any nearer). The need became even greater when the UN forces were quickly rolled back into a perimeter around Pusan.

Valley Forge (CV-45) and CVG-5 (Air Group Five) were the only US Navy carrier force in the Western Pacific at the start of the Korean War, and only HMS *Triumph* was in the vicinity to give immediate

Below: Rocket-firing F4U Corsairs warm up on the flight deck of the USS *Bunker Hill*. Of all the fighters built during World War Two, the 'Bent Winged Bird' remained in production the longest, the 12,571st and final model being built on Christmas Eve 1952, and it was one of several wartime types still in frontline service at the outbreak of the Korean War in 1950. While jets were about 100 mph faster than Corsairs or Skyraiders, the early jets could not haul as great a warload over a long distance, and they were slow to respond from when the throttle was advanced to the time the engine 'spooled up' sufficiently to accelerate the aircraft. This delay could prove fatal if a jet had to be waved off a landing at the last moment. Corsairs, with their huge variable-pitch propellers and Double Wasps, permitted fast acceleration. (*USN via Hunter Reinburg*)

Above: TBM-3A Avengers and a Grumman F9F Panther aboard the USS *Coral Sea* (CVB43), one of three Midway-class heavily armoured battle carriers ordered in 1942–3, which was commissioned on 1 October 1947. The Avenger remained in service until June 1954. (*National Archives via Peter C. Smith*)

support. However, CVG-5 was the most experienced jet air group in the Navy. VF-51 'Screaming Eagles' had been the first to operate jets from a carrier and were the first to be equipped with the Grumman F9F Panther. In January 1950 a carrier's air group composition had been changed from three fighter and two attack squadrons to four fighter (VF) (two F4U-4 Corsair and two F9F-3 Panther) and one attack (VA) squadron (AD-4 Skyraiders). Each group comprised ninety aircraft, or eighteen in each squadron.

F9F-3s had replaced VF-51's FJ-1 Furys in May 1949. The Screaming Eagles, as they were known, thus became the first Panther squadron, and the first to operate jets from a carrier when VF-51 began operations from *Boxer* in September. When the Korean War erupted, VF-51 were aboard *Valley Forge* in the Pacific. On 3 July 1950 Panthers were the first jet fighters in the US Navy to go into action when thirty from VF-51 provided top cover for the carrier's Skyraiders and F4U Corsairs, which bombed targets near the North Korean capital, Pyongyang. Two F9F-3 pilots, Lt(jg) L. H. Plog and Ensign E. W. Brown, each destroyed a Yak-9 fighter in addition to destroying two more on the ground.

The carrier *Sicily* arrived off Korea and began operations using USMC F4U-4s on 2 August, and was joined on 6 August by the *Badoeng Strait*. In December *Bataan* arrived, and in 1951 these were joined by the escort carriers *Bairoko* (CVE 115) and *Rendova*. After World War Two the USN had been consistently pruned, and many carriers were either mothballed or undermanned. It was for the latter reason that the fast attack Essex-class carrier *Philippine Sea* (CV-47), commissioned 11 May 1946, had to remain at Quonset Point in a reduced-commission state. On 24 May 1950 she sailed from Norfolk, Virginia for San Diego, California, arriving on 10 June. On 5 July, fifteen days after the North Koreans crossed the 38th Parallel, *Philippine Sea* was ordered to Hawaii and ultimately Korea with Air Group 11 (CVG-11), commanded by Cdr W. 'Sully' Vogel Jr. VF-111 and VF-112, equipped with the F9F-2, VF-113 and VF-114's F4U Corsair fighter-bombers, VA-115's AD-4B Skyraiders, and detachments from Composite Squadron 3 (CV-3) equipped with F4U-5N night-fighters/-5P photo-reconnaissance models, and AD-4Bs (VC-11 with AD-4Bs, VC-61 with F4U-4s, and VC-35), were embarked. A single HO3 S-1 from HU-1 was also on board and would be used for planeguard and utility duties.

Philippine Sea finally joined Task Force 77 on 31 July 1950. She arrived in Buckner Bay, Okinawa, on 1 August to begin work-ups for combat with *Valley Forge* in attacks on Korea from both the Yellow Sea and the Sea of Japan. CVG-11 launched its first attacks on 5 August when Lt-Cdr William T. Amen led VF-111 in attacks on airfields at Mokpo, Kwangju and Kusan, while eight F9F Panthers of VF-112 and twelve Corsairs of VF-114 hit rail and road bridges in the Mokpo–Kwangju area. The F4Us destroyed a bridge and damaged two dams south of Iri before strafing warehouses, sampans and junks on the way home. Between 7 and 13 August *Philippine Sea* supported the UN counter-offensive in the Masan Sector as the North Koreans attempted to break through the Pusan Perimeter. VF-113 lost two F4Us

Below: AD-4B Skyraider of VA-115 taking off from the USS *Philippine Sea* (CV-47). Before sailing from San Diego, California on 5 July 1950, she embarked Air Group 11 (CVG-11); two F9F-2B squadrons, VF-111 and VF-112; two F4U-4 fighter-bomber squadrons, VF-113 and VF-114; an AD-4 Skyraider squadron, VA-115; plus detachments from CV-3, VC-11, VC-35 and VC-61. CVG-11 had not yet finished its training cycle, as its two jet squadrons had just received its F9F Panthers (right), the first of the Navy carrier-borne jet fighters. The F9F-2 remained the Navy's first-line jet fighter throughout the first year of the Korean War. Arriving at Oahu, Hawaii on 10 July 1950, CV-47 conducted intensive CarQuals (Carrier Qualifications). *Philippine Sea* anchored in Buckner Bay in Okinawa on

1 August 1950 and prepared for battle 5 August 1950. In the wardroom, Rear-Admiral Edward C. Ewen and thirty-five-year-old Cdr W. 'Sully' Vogel Jr, a veteran of aerial combat in the Pacific in World War Two, CAG 11, addressed the pilots prior to launch. Lt-Cdr William T. Amen led VF-111's first launch, taking his men to sweep airfields at Mokpo, Kwangju and Kusan. VF-112's Panthers, two divisions of four aircraft, likewise hit targets in the Mokpo–Kwangju area. VF-114's twelve F4U-4s destroyed a bridge, damaged two dams south of Iri and blasted various targets of opportunity such as warehouses, sampans and junks on the way home.
(*Roland H. Baker*)

Above: During *Philippine Sea*'s first tour of duty off Korea, 5 August 1950 to 15 February 1951, VF-113 and VF-114's F4U-4s were embarked, and in this picture one of them has lowered its arrestor hook preparatory to landing on board. *Philippine Sea*'s pilots joined those from CVG-5 on board *Valley Forge* in flying combat operations against North Korean forces attempting to break through the Pusan Perimeter. The carrier aviators conducted close air support (CAS) and interdiction of enemy supply lines as CV-47 operated off the south and eastern coasts of Korea. Tragedy struck VF-113 on the first day when, fifteen miles south of Kunsan, two F4U-4s collided during a strafing run. Ensign J. F. Kail crashed immediately, while Ensign G. T. Farnsworth nursed his crippled plane out over the sea, where he ditched, to be picked up that same afternoon. Next day, a VF-113 pilot pressed home his attack at such low level that his Corsair took major damage from his own bomb blast, but he made it back to his carrier and a safe landing. *(Roland H. Baker)*

which collided during a strafing run while providing close air support and interdiction of enemy supply lines. Ensign J. F. Krail was killed, while Ensign G. T. Farnsworth nursed his damaged Corsair out to sea where he ditched. Farnsworth was picked up that same afternoon.

On 16 August, after replenishing in Japan, *Philippine Sea* sent its aircraft over Korea again. On the 19th, thirty-seven F4Us and Skyraiders from the *Philippine Sea* and *Valley Forge*, escorted by Panthers, scored eight direct hits on a large steel railway bridge west of Seoul which had withstood days of heavy bombing by B-29s of the 19th Bomb Group, including one strike which saw fifty-four tons of bombs explode around it. Cdr W. 'Sully' Vogel Jr, CAG 11, leading VF-114, was shot down by AA fire on his second pass. The Pacific combat veteran baled out but his parachute failed to open properly. Gen. George E. Stratemeyer, CIC, FEAF (Far East Air Force), had promised a case of Scotch whisky to the first crew to destroy the bridge. The spans of the bridge fell into the Han river that night before B-29s of the 19th Bomb Group could drop their special

2,000 and 4,000lb bombs the following morning, but honours were declared even, with the 19th and Navy Air Group 111 both receiving cases of whisky!

On 15 September General Douglas MacArthur launched Operation 'Chromite', using amphibious landings behind the enemy lines at Inchon with the majority of the air cover provided by F4Us and Skyraiders from *Valley Forge*, *Philippine Sea* and *Boxer* (recently arrived from the USA), and Seafires and Fireflies from HMS *Triumph*. Navy and USMC fighter-bombers strafed and bombed positions along the Inchon waterfront prior to the main landing. By midnight the operation had achieved all the objectives. The North Koreans fell back in the face of the offensive and the Navy pilots went in search of interdiction targets. During this period Lt Carl C. Dace made the first combat ejection from a jet fighter when he banged out after his Panther was hit by AA fire during a ground attack run over North Korea. By 28 September the Communists were in full retreat, and by 9 October American troops had crossed the 38th Parallel and were heading for Pyongyang.

China entered the war on the North Korean side

and on 1 November American aircraft were confronted by the MiG-15 for the first time. An area 100 miles deep between Sinuiju on the Yalu and Sinanju on the Chongchon River soon became known as 'MiG Alley'. For three consecutive days, beginning 9 November, F4Us and AD-4s from *Valley Forge*, *Leyte* and *Philippine Sea* hit bridges on the Yalu, destroying a road bridge at Sinuiju and two more at Hyesanjin. The Grumman was outclassed by the MiG, but the superior experience of the Navy pilots gave them the edge. On 10 November a Panther from *Philippine Sea* was the first US Navy jet to down another jet aircraft when Lt-Cdr W. T. Amen, CO of VF-111, flying a VF-112 Panther, destroyed a MiG-15 near Sinuiju.

On 28 December *Philippine Sea* and *Leyte* arrived in Yokosuka, Japan, for rest and replenishment after fifty-two consecutive days on the line. On 8 January 1951 the two carriers, together with *Valley Forge*, were on station again, helping to repel the Chinese New Year offensive. Aircraft from the *Philippine Sea* attacked enemy positions until 1 February, when the carrier replenished again in Japan, and from 12 February to 13 March. Four days later *Philippine Sea*

and *Valley Forge* returned to Yokosaka and an exchange of air groups began. CVG-11 disembarked and three Corsair squadrons, VF-24, 63 and 64, and VA-65, equipped with the Skyraider, and the usual Composite Squadron detachments, were embarked from Air Group Two aboard *Valley Forge*. After seeing further action *Philippine Sea* sailed for the USA on 2 June 1951.

Meanwhile, on 2 April, Panthers relinquished their escort role and carried out their first ground attack mission in Korea when two F9F-2Bs of VF-191 from *Princeton*, each carrying four 250lb and two 100lb GP bombs, bombed a rail bridge near Songjin. Attack and counter-attack continued for weeks, until on 31 May Operation 'Strangle', an air interdiction campaign using the 5th AF, 1st Marine Air Wing and Task Force 77, was mounted against road and rail routes and bridges in north-east Korea. On 18 August aircraft from Task Force 77 attacked twenty-seven bridges and rail lines running to the east coast. Samdong-ni to Kowon was soon christened Death Valley by Navy aviators, who grew to respect the enemy AA fire in the area. *Essex* arrived on station joining Task Force 77, and on 23 August its

Below: Two five-inch HVAR (High Velocity Aerial Rockets) and two longer, modified with 6.5-inch diameter anti-tank (ATAR) 'Ram rockets' for penetrating the T-34 tanks used by North Korea, are fitted to the underwing of a F4U-4. The standard five-inch warhead was found to be too small to damage the Soviet-built tanks used by the Communists. On 9 August 1950 CAG Sully Vogel flew with VF-114, leading a

strike against the Riken Metal Company in Seoul, Korea, using 500lb bombs and rockets. Vogel's flight hit the target 'very effectively'. Vogel led another VF-114 strike on 13 August, this time against targets near Pyongyang, the North Korean capital.
(*Roland H. Baker*)

Above: An AD-4B of VA-115 is catapulted off the flight deck. On 9 August, later in the day, VA-115's Skyraiders teamed up with VF-114's Corsairs to blast the marshalling yards and the Standard Oil Company warehouses in Seoul, leaving the latter burning, and knocked out several boxcars and a locomotive.
(Roland H. Baker)

McDonnell F2H-2 Banshees made their combat debut for VF-172 with an escort for the B-29s. Late in 1951 two future astronauts made the headlines. On 23 October Lt Walter M. Schirra, USN, shot down a MiG while on an exchange with the 136th FB Wing. On a later mission, Ensign Neil A. Armstrong, from *Essex*, baled out and was rescued after his Panther was hit during a strafing run near Wonsan.

Early in March 1952 Task Force 77 was part of Operation 'Saturate', a sustained offensive aimed at short sections of railway line to deny their use to the enemy. By April Task Force 77 comprised *Valley Forge* with Air Task Group 1 (ATG-1) (VF-52/111/194/653 and four detachments) embarked; *Philippine Sea* (which, after an overhaul, had rejoined TF77 on 3 February), with Air Group 11 (VF-112/3/4/5 and four detachments); *Boxer*, with Air Group 2 (VF-24/63/64/65 and three detachments); and *Princeton*, with Air Group 19 (VF-191/192/193/195 and four detachments). (At the end of the war *Lake Champlain* was on station in place of *Valley Forge*.)

On 16 June aircraft from Task Force 77 pasted Kowon, supported by an effective chaff cloud to 'snow' enemy radar-controlled AA guns. Beginning on 23 June the UN air forces began a sustained offensive against the North's four principal hydroelectric plants, with a first attack on the Suiho generating plant in MiG Alley, forty miles from Antung, where 250 MiGs were based. Some thirty-five skyraiders from *Boxer*'s VA-65, *Princeton*'s VA-195 and *Philippine Sea*'s VA-115, together with thirty-five flak-suppression F9F Panthers from *Boxer*, *Princeton* and *Philippine Sea*, set out, with eighty-four USAF Sabres as top cover. Thirty-one Skyraiders carried two 2,000lb bombs and a 1,000-pounder, while the other four carried two 2,000lb bombs and a 'survival bomb' containing survival gear. The Panthers took the North Koreans completely by surprise and dropped their 250lb GP bombs and strafed the eighty AA emplacements around Suiho at will. Then the Skyraiders delivered more than eighty-five tons of bombs in less than two minutes on the Suiho powerhouse. One AD-4, from VA-115, flown by Lt(jg) M. K. Lake, was one of five hit by AA fire, and he made a forced landing at Kimpo. After the Navy departed, 124 F-84G Thunderjet fighter-bombers hit the plant. Later, USAF and naval aircraft from *Boxer*, *Princeton* and *Bon Homme Richard* attacked Fusen and Kyosen. Suiho, Fusen and the two other plants were obliterated. The feared interception by the MiGs never occurred – they beat it across the Yalu to the safety of Manchuria.

On 11 July 1952 Task Force 77, part of a massive USMC, USAF and Royal Naval airborne force,

Above: The single Sikorsky HO3S-1 (UP-29) of Helicopter Utility Squadron One (HU-1) used for planeguard and utility duties aboard the USS *Philippine Sea* during the carrier's first cruise off Korea, 5 August 1950 to 1 February 1951. HU-1 helicopters were nicknamed 'Angels' for their role as SAR aircraft for downed pilots. (*Roland H. Baker*)

Below: *Philippine Sea* pictured in harbour in Japan during one of her seven replenishments at Sasebo and Yokosuka, August 1950 to May 1951. CV-47 made her first replenishment at Sasebo, 14–15 August 1950, and then returned to the east coast of Korea, commencing CAS for hard-pressed UN forces and bombing key bridges near Seoul on the 16th. Next day, VF-113's F4U-4s caught a twenty-truck convoy with a cargo of artillery on the road south of Songjin and obliterated it. At 1531 hours on 19 August, *Philippine Sea* launched eight F4U-4s from VF-114 led by Cdr Sully Vogel on a strike near Seoul. While the four-plane CAP (Combat Air Patrol) element encountered no enemy aircraft, the four strike aircraft hit a bridge span with one 500-pounder on the first pass. Sully Vogel came around again for a second pass, but enemy AA fire hit his Corsair and set it on fire. Vogel baled out of the burning Corsair and pilots saw his 'chute stream, but it did not open and his body hurtled to the ground. Vogel left a widow and five children. Although CVG-11 pilots destroyed the Han River bridge near Seoul that day, little solace lay in the feat. Next day, Ensign C. L. Smith of VF-112 died when his Panther crashed and burned near Sariwon. *Philippine Sea* cleared Korean waters on 20 August and the next day, as the carrier lay anchored at Sasebo, a memorial service was held for Sully Vogel and Ensign Smith. (*Roland H. Baker*)

Above: TBM Avenger on a sortie from Atsugi, Japan. This was how Richard H. Baker, a World War Two Pacific Hellcat pilot and Assistant Air Intelligence Officer aboard the *Philippine Sea* at the time of Korea, got his air time. Avengers were fitted out as transports for COD operations off Korea. (*Roland H. Baker*)

Below: A Panther jet comes in to land aboard its carrier against a backdrop of the setting sun. CF-47 finished her replenishment at Sasebo on 25 August and returned to the east coast of Korea. On the 27th, CVG-11 hit shipping in Wonsan Harbour, damaging what pilots claimed as a 'destroyer escort' with rockets and cannon fire, and two 'gunboats' by strafing. Between 26 August and 4 September 1950, CVG-11 pilots claimed destruction of a 'fleet type minelayer' and four patrol craft at Wonsan. They conducted emergency CAS in defence of the Pusan Perimeter and destroyed key bridges along the North Korean lines of communication. *Philippine Sea*'s aviators also discovered the enemy's major staging base at Kangge and photographed Inchon prior to the amphibious landing there. Replenishing at Sasebo, 5–11 September 1950, CV-47 launched pre-invasion strikes in the Inchon–Seoul area, 12–14 September, and furnished air cover for the Inchon landing on the 15th. In this bold thrust, the First Marine Division took the enemy by surprise, captured the port of Inchon and, with the Army's 7th Infantry Division, captured Seoul and Kimpo airfield, serving communist supply routes to the south. Breaking the enemy stranglehold on Pusan, UN forces seized the initiative. (*Roland H. Baker*)

Left: LSO (Landing Signals Officer) and other crew aboard CV-47 directing operations for landing. Between 16 September and 3 October 1950 CVG-11 furnished 'deep support' of allied forces and bombed supply routes and airfields from Seoul to Pyongyang, the North Korean capital, before retiring to Sasebo on 4 October for a five-day respite. Early in this period, on 17 September, twenty-five-year-old Ensign Edward D. Jackson Jr, of VF-112, while pressing a low-level strafing run south of Seoul, flew through high-tension cables strung across the Han River. His F9F sustained extensive damage and he suffered painful facial lacerations and partial blindness. His wingman, Ensign Dayl E. Crow, 'talked' him to the ship and into the groove. The LSO took it from there and brought him safely on board in a blind landing, as Jackson caught the number five wire. (*Roland H. Baker*)

participated in Operation 'Pressure Pump', the largest air attack so far, against thirty military targets in Pyongyang. Some 1,254 sorties were flown for the loss of just three aircraft. On 29 August an even mightier force, including USMC Panthers and F4Us and Navy Corsairs, Banshees and Panthers from *Boxer* and *Essex*, returned to devastate the capital. On 1 September 1952 Task Force 77 dispatched the largest naval air strike of the war when aircraft from *Essex*, *Princeton* and *Bon Homme Richard* left the synthetic oil refinery at Aoji in ruins.

The Navy's last great all-out offensive was in May–June 1953 when carrier-borne aircraft flew ground-support missions for seven days. On 14–15 June Task Force 77, comprising *Boxer*, *Philippine Sea* (now returned from a sojourn to California and redesignated an attack aircraft carrier (CVA-47) with Air Group Nine from *Essex* embarked), *Princeton* and *Lake Champlain*, flew round-the-clock missions in support of the First ROK Corps' attacks to regain 'Anchor Hill'. Then, on 27 July, the Communists signed the Armistice and the thirty-eight-month war was over.

Peace reigned once again in the Land of the Morning Calm.

Below: Korean winters could be hell, as this shot of frozen F4U-4s of VF-113 and VF-114, F9F-2B Panthers of VF-111 and VF-112, and AD-4B Skyraiders of VA-115 on the deck of *Philippine Sea* in the winter of 1950–1 shows. (*Roland H. Baker*)

Above: Ordnancemen bring out their bombs to load on the wings of Skyraiths. During nine months of operations, August 1950 to May 1951, CV-47 expended 5,985 tons of bombs and rockets, and 1,335 tons of napalm. (*Roland H. Baker*)

Below: UNREP (Underway Replenishment) taking place between a supply ship and a carrier of Task Force 77 in very rough waters off Korea. (*Roland H. Baker*)

Above: F9F-2B Panther of VF-112 taxies in on *Philippine Sea*. November 1950 marked the massive intervention by Chinese Communist 'volunteers', who swarmed south to aid the North Koreans. The Chinese Air Force introduced a new element to the war, with MiG-15s, which posed a serious threat to the prop-driven ADs and F4Us. The Chinese intervention soon cut short *Philippine Sea*'s stay in Japan, and she sailed on 6 November, rejoining TF77 on the 9th. On that day, her planes bombed bridges spanning the Yalu River and supply concentrations in Hungnam, Songjin and Chongjin. The Panther was the first Navy jet to down another jet aircraft when Lt-Cdr William T. Amen, CAG VF-111, flying a VF-112 F9F, destroyed a MiG-15 during a raid on bridges at Sinuiju on the Yalu on 9 November. Over the next few weeks CVG-11, as well as planes from *Leyte* (CV-32) and *Valley Forge* (CV-45), pounded the enemy. On 17 November, CV-47 joined *Leyte* in sending planes to drop both bridges across the Yalu and Hyosanjin. Lt(jg) Thomas J. Hudner, of VF-32, flying from *Leyte* on 4 December 1950, was the only Corsair pilot awarded the Medal of Honor during the Korean War. Hudner deliberately made a wheels-up landing behind enemy lines to go to the aid of downed wingman Ensign Jesse L. Brown (the Navy's first black aviator), who was trapped in his burning F4U-4, but his valiant effort was in vain.
(*Roland H. Baker*)

Above: AD-4Bs of VA-115 queue on deck for launching as an LSO directs operations amidst their whirling propellers. On 26 November 1950, Red Chinese forces smashed into the 'greatly extended' UN forces in a surprise assault, driving a deep wedge between 8th Army and 10th Corps. The spectre of isolation and annihilation loomed large as allied troops pulled back before the enemy onslaught. Between 2 and 25 December *Philippine Sea*'s planes conducted CAS in the Chosin Reservoir area, covering the successful extraction of ground forces (most notably the 1st Marine Division) to Hungnam and evacuation. Completing these operations on Christmas Day 1950, CV-47 retired and reached Sasebo on the 26th, remaining until 7 January 1951. On the 8th CV-47 rejoined TF77 and supported UN operations around the 38th Parallel, attacking enemy supply routes on the east coast of Korea until 1 February 1951. She was detached that day, and she sailed for Yokosuka, arriving on the 3rd for a week's sojourn. On 12 February the carrier again operated off Korea's east coast, providing interdiction and CAS until 13 March 1951.
(*Roland H. Baker*)

Below: A plane captain smiles for Roland H. Baker's camera while attending to a F4U-4.

Above right: Before the strike can begin, the planes on the carriers have to be refuelled and rearmed. Here, an armourer carrying belts of ammunition for waiting aircraft walks purposefully across the flight deck. CV-47 expended 2,747,000 machine-gun and cannon ammunition, August 1950 to May 1951. An ominous portent of things to come occurred on 30 September 1950 when VF-113's Corsair pilots sighted their first Soviet-built MiG-15 jet fighter in the skies some thirty miles north-west of Seoul. *Philippine Sea* resumed operations, 10 October 1950, providing air cover for the invasion of Wonsan, as well as bombing enemy supply centres and routes from Wonsan to Chonglin. Ship and air group returned to Sasebo on 23 October, resting in Japan until November 1950.
(*Roland H. Baker*)

Above: F9F-5 piloted by Ensign Pyle of VF-781 heads for the barrier aboard the USS *Oriskany* (CV-34) on 29 March 1951. The Allison A33-A-16 used on the F9F-4 was replaced by a Pratt & Whitney J48-P-2 (modelled on the Rolls-Royce Tay) on the F9F-5, which differed from previous models in having a higher pointed tail. By December 1952 619 F9F-5s had been accepted. Of the 826 Navy and USMC jets deployed to Korea, no fewer than 715 were Panthers, and they flew about 78,000 combat sorties. (*USN*)

Above: Between 26 March and 2 April 1951, at Okusuka, the *Philippine Sea* disembarked CVG-11 and embarked three F4U-4 Corsair squadrons: VF-24 ('402', a yellow-tipped VF-24 aircraft, nearest the camera), VF-63 and VF-64, as well as VA-65's Skyraiders and the usual composite squadron detachments, all from CVG-2, which previously had served onboard *Valley Forge*. VF-63, operating from *Boxer*, 15 September to 22 October 1950, and *Valley Forge*, 16 December 1950 to 2 June 1951, flew 1,055 sorties and blazed a trail of destruction, killing over 2,000 enemy troops, destroying or damaging twenty-seven gun positions, and obliterating fifty vehicles and one tank, eighteen supply and fuel dumps, 1,156 troop shelters, 450 buildings, one locomotive, 146 rail cars, forty-five bridges, sixteen warehouses, 114 oxen and horses, and five junks! (*Roland H. Baker*)

Above: A VA-65 armourer adjusts the 20mm gun of an AD-4 Skyraider at sea. All 372 AD-4s built were fitted with four 20mm guns with 200 rounds. Faulty guns caused by the extremely low temperatures at altitude were a common and vexing problem. (*Roland H. Baker*)

Below: F-4U-4s of VF-24, VF-63, VF-64 and (right) AD-4Bs of VA-65 aboard the *Philippine Sea*. Rejoining TF77 on 4 April 1951, the fighting *Philippine Sea* resumed operations in the Sea of Japan until the 8th, when she and her screen sailed for Formosa to counter Red Chinese threats against the island. After a show of force off the Chinese coast and over the northern part of Formosa, 11–13 April 1951, CV-47 returned north, giving support to UN ground forces, 16 April to 3 May. (*Roland H. Baker*)

Left: Drop tanks filled with napalm about to be loaded on aircraft aboard the *Philippine Sea*. Napalm, or napalmgel, is a petrol thickened with a compound made from aluminium, naphthenic and palmitic acids, to which white phosphorus is added for ignition. Behind is the single HO3S-1 (UP-29) utility helicopter, used mainly for planeguard duties. (*Roland H. Baker*)

Below: AD-4B Skyraider of VA-65 carrying rockets and two drop tanks filled with napalm for a raid on North Korean targets. AD-4s could carry three 2,000lb bombs, torpedoes or drop tanks on the main pylons, while outer-wing stations were used for 500lb bombs or rockets, with a maximum capacity of up to 6,500lb operating from a carrier. (*Roland H. Baker*)

Below: F4U-4 Corsair '211' of VF-24, flaps down, alights on the flight deck of the *Philippine Sea*, spring 1951. (*Roland H. Baker*)

Above: F4U-4 '410' of VF-24, its wings folded upwards just after landing aboard the USS *Philippine Sea*. (*Roland H. Baker*)

Below: F4U-4 '115' of VF-64 takes off for a strike over Korea. (*Roland H. Baker*)

Left: A smiling ordnanceman with a bomb on his shoulder goes about his work on the busy flight deck beside F4U-4s of VF-64. Detached from TF77 on 3 May 1951, *Philippine Sea* returned to Yokosuka three days later. The North Korean spring offensive, however, soon pulled the carrier back to the line. (*Roland H. Baker*)

Below: F4U-4 '113' of VF-64 with empty weapons racks and wings folded upwards, taxies down the flight deck of the *Philippine Sea* after another strike over Korea. (*Roland H. Baker*)

Above: An F4U-4 of VF-24 taxies away after landing aboard *Philippine Sea* as three more Corsairs pass overhead. CV-47 provided close air support for the continually hard-pressed UN forces, 17–30 May 1951. From August 1950 to May 1951, she conducted 7,727 offensive sorties, 2,660 defence, and 1,856 miscellaneous sorties. Her close air support had been delivered in areas ranging from a few miles in advance of the front lines to only a few yards. CF-47 detached from TF77 on 30 May 1951 and departed for the west coast of America on 2 June 1951, passing beneath the Golden Gate bridge on 9 June 1951. She moored at NAS Alameda, California, to a tumultuous welcome. Following a quick trip to San Diego, *Philippine Sea* sailed for Hunter's Point Naval Shipyard at San Francisco, arriving 21 June 1951, nearly one year after her hasty departure for the war zone. Upon completion of her overhaul, in the autumn and winter of 1951 CV-47 conducted CarQuals in the San Diego area. Again with CVG-11 embarked, she sailed for the Far East, on 31 December 1951.
(*Roland H. Baker*)

Below: An AD-4 of VA-115 loaded with bombs is flagged off the flight deck of the *Philippine Sea*. On 23 June 1952, for the first time in eighteen months, four fleet carriers – *Philippine Sea*, *Bon Homme Richard*, *Boxer* (CV-21) and *Princeton* (CV-37) – were operating together off the Korean coast. At 1400 hours on 23 June 1953 the four carriers commenced the biggest strike of the war at the time, against the hitherto untouched hydroelectric plant at Suiho, a major source for Manchurian industry. Altogether, thirty-five Skyraiders from *Boxer*'s VA-65, *Princeton*'s VA-195 and *Philippine Sea*'s VA-115 took part. Thirty-one of the ADs hauled a pair of 2,000-pounders and one 1,000-pounder, while the other four each carried two 2,000-pounders and one 'bomb' containing survival gear if anyone was shot down.
(*Roland H. Baker*)

Left: Senior officers aboard the island watch pensively as aircraft are launched for operations. From 4 to 20 February 1952 CV-47 launched nearly continuous air strikes in an effort to impede North Korean rail traffic. Other frequent targets for nearly 450 tons of ordnance expended during this period included transportation, communications, industrial and supply facilities. Only a task for replenishment or bad weather kept aircraft idle, and then only for a short period of time. After R&R in Yokosuka, 22 February to 17 March 1952, CV-47 resumed her interdiction and CAS tasks on 20 March. After repairs in Yokosuka, 16 April to 13 May, the carrier launched strikes on the 14th. Mid-May to 4 June 1952, she launched 1,180 sorties against transportation and communications targets, as well as blasting industrial and supply facilities, in particular the North Korean railway system.
(*Roland H. Baker*)

Below: F4U-5NL night-fighter Corsair of VC-3 all-weather combat fighter squadron, fitted with an APS-19 radar intercept scanner in a housing on the starboard wing. In July 1953, Lt Guy P. Bordelon Jr, and a fellow pilot of VC-3 aboard the USS *Princeton*, were dispatched to K-6 airfield south of Seoul to try to counter 'Heckling' missions flown by NKAF Yak-18 training aircraft, which were proving more than just a nuisance to USMC operations. (On the night of 16/17 July a NKAF Yak-18 bombed a fuel dump at Inchon, destroying five million gallons of fuel.) In three

night missions over a three-week period Bordelon destroyed five 'Bed Check Charlies', as they were known, to become the only Navy ace in Korea. Apart from night air-superiority sorties, F4U-5s often guided Skyraiders to their targets, dropping flares and leading the attack. VC-3 detachments served aboard nine of the twelve carriers that operated off Korea. (Colloquially, in the USN those who remain ashore from those that deploy are known as the 'Palace Guard'.)
(*Roland H. Baker*)

Below: Lt Dauphin climbs into the cockpit of F2H-2 Banshee BuNo124974 aboard CV-9 in Korean waters in October 1951 while crewmen swarm over the 'Banjo' making last-minute preparations for flight. Guns are being checked, the nose-wheel dolly disconnected, screens have been removed and all external points noted on the check-list. The F2H was powered by two 3,250lb thrust Westinghouse J34 turbojets. F2H-2 Banshees from VF-172 aboard the USS *Essex* first went into combat in Korea on 23 August 1951.
(*McDonnell Corp*)

Opposite above: Skyraiders on board *Philippine Sea* silhouetted against a Pacific sunset. During the carrier's last deployment of the war, 31 January to 27 July 1953, CVA-47 launched 7,243 sorties (including forty-nine on the last day prior to the truce) and logged just over 7,700 traps. CVG-9's planes had delivered almost 9,000,000lb of bombs and fired almost 386,000 rounds of .50 calibre and 619,000 rounds of 20mm ammunition. CV-47 sailed to San Diego in August 1952, returning to the Far East redesignated as an attack aircraft carrier (CVA-47) in December 1952, with CVG-9 embarked. Operations were carried out until 27 July 1953, the day of the armistice, when, ironically, CVG-9 was due to rotate home. CVA-47 reached NAS Alameda, California on 14 August 1953. Only twelve years old, *Philippine Sea* was placed out of commission, in reserve, on 22 December 1958, and in May 1959 she became an 'auxiliary aircraft carrier transport' before being stricken on 1 December 1969 and being sold for scrap in 1971. (*Roland H. Baker*)

Above: In addition, thirty-five F9Fs from *Boxer*'s VF-24, *Princeton*'s VF-191 and *Philippine Sea*'s VF-112 flew cover on 23 June. Two dozen of the Panthers carried two 250lb GP bombs and a full ammunition load. Providing top cover over MiG Alley were eighty-four USAF F-86 Sabres. Taking the enemy completely by surprise, the flak-suppression F9Fs led the way while the ADs reversed course and commenced their runs. With the Suiho powerhouse providing an excellent aiming point (a building 80ft by 500ft), the Navy strike delivered more than eighty-five tons of bombs in less than two minutes, attacking the powerhouse and nearby transformer yard and penstocks. They cleared the area with only five planes hit by AA fire, and all but one returned to their carriers. The exception was an AD-4 from VA-115. The pilot, Lt(jg) M. K. Lake, managed to make a wheels-up landing at Kimpo airfield near Seoul.
(*Grumman*)

Above: F9Fs, AD Skyraiders and F4U-4s warming up on the deck of the *Bon Homme Richard* (CVA-31), or 'Bonny Dick' as it was affectionately known, for another strike on Thanksgiving Day, November 1952 against targets in Korea.
(*USN*)

CHAPTER 4
AIR WAR VIETNAM, 1964–73

The Korean War had shaken the military might of America, and it led to far-reaching changes in the equipment it would need to fight any similar war anywhere in the world. The Navy replaced its F9F Panther and F2H Banshee straight-winged jets with the F-4 Phantom, and the Vought F-8 Crusader became the standard carrier-based fighter, although propeller-driven aircraft, like the Douglas A-1 Skyraider, still had a role to play. Ed Heinmann's Douglas A-4 Skyhawk was designed to replace the Skyraider and fulfil a multiplicity of roles for the Navy, including interceptor and nuclear weapons carrier, but for a while both aircraft served alongside each other when war broke out in south-east Asia.

In July 1954 the Republic of South Vietnam was created, using the 17th Parallel to separate it from the Communist North. However, Ho Chi Minh's Viet Minh forces, led by General Giap, planned to take over control of the South using a new Communist guerrilla force called the Viet Cong (VC) or National Liberation Front (NLF). The VC campaign increased in intensity in 1957 and finally, in 1960, Premier Diem appealed to the United States for help. In 1961 'special advisers' were sent in, and later President Lyndon B. Johnson began the first moves which would lead to total American involvement in Vietnam.

When in 1964 two Crusaders were brought down during a reconnaissance mission over Laos, the USAF flew a retaliatory strike on 9 June against AAA sites. On 2 August the Seventh Fleet was involved in an incident with North Vietnamese torpedo boats in the Gulf of Tonkin. A flight of four F-8E Crusaders of

Below: When the Korean War ended there were twenty-four Navy Skyraider squadrons. By September 1955 this had risen to twenty-nine, and three versions of the AD-5 and AD-6 ground-support single-seater aircraft were in production (all told, no fewer than twenty-two versions of the Skyraider were built). The four-seat AD-5W (218 built) was an AEW aircraft (BuNo139569 of VAW-12 is seen here) fitted with a ventral APS-20 'guppy' radome for over-the-horizon detection. Two radar operators were carried within the fuselage, necessitating the removal of dive-brakes. An experimental clear-coated natural metal finish with black codes was applied to selected aircraft within certain squadrons and was in use 29 April 1952 to 16 February 1955, when it was cancelled because of problems with corrosion. Under the 1962 Tri-Service designation system, the 'Able Dog' 5W became the EA-1E. (*Roland H. Baker*)

Above: Swept wings and tail were added to the standard Grumman Panther fuselage, and the F9F-6 Cougar was born in 1951. The much improved F9F-8, with an air-refuelling probe in the nose of a longer fuselage, and with longer range, appeared in December 1953. F9F-8s (601 were delivered, April 1954 to March 1957) were first deployed overseas with VA-46 in July 1956. Among the last Cougars were 110 F9F-8Ps fitted with seven cameras (delivered August 1955 to July 1957), and these served photographic squadrons until February 1960. Here, an F9F-8P of VFP-62 shares the deck with F9F-8 BuNo141665 from VA-44, about to be catapulted off the carrier deck. F9F-8Bs were finally phased out in 1958–9, while F9-8Ps were the last Cougars to serve a fleet squadron, being retained by VFP-62 until February 1960. (*Roland H. Baker*)

Above: After more than ten years in production, Vought stopped building Corsairs in December 1952, and production switched to the F7U-1 Cutlass at a new plant at Dallas, Texas. However, five early F7U-1s crashed, killing three test pilots, the planned F7U-2 was cancelled, and the F7U-3 (51-29549 seen here) did not reach the fleet until 1954, with VC-3. F7U-3s saw only limited fleet service, and they were withdrawn in November 1957. (*Vought*)

Above: Equally unsuccessful was the underpowered McDonnell F-3H Demon, which first flew on 7 August 1951. Six test aircraft were lost in eleven accidents, and four pilots were killed. It was not until March 1956 that Demons finally entered service, and the much-maligned interceptor served for just eight and a half years. (*McDonnell*)

VF-53 from the *Ticonderoga* made several strafing runs on the boats, firing their 20mm cannon and Zuni unguided rockets. Two days later Crusaders, A-4 Skyhawks and Skyraiders bombed and rocketed four large PT boat bases along the North Vietnamese coast, destroying or damaging twenty-five torpedo boats. Lt(jg) Everett Alvarez, an A-4C pilot from the *Constellation*, was shot down and he became the first POW of the war.

In February 1965 the Viet Cong stepped up its guerrilla war and the first American casualties in Vietnam occurred when the VC attacked US installations in the South. In retaliation, the order was given for a strike from carriers in the Gulf of Tonkin. 'Flaming Dart I', as the strike was code-named, saw forty-nine aircraft launched from the decks of the *Hancock* and *Coral Sea* against VC installations at Dong Hoi, while the *Ranger* sent thirty-four aircraft to bomb Vit Thu Lu. One A-4E from the *Coral Sea* was shot down and the pilot drowned. On 11 February three Navy aircraft were lost in the 'Flaming Dart' strike on Vietnamese barracks at Chanh Hoa.

In March Operation 'Rolling Thunder', an air offensive against North Vietnam, was launched and the Navy's first strike took place on 18 March when aircraft from the *Coral Sea* and *Hancock* bombed supply dumps at Phu Van and Vinh Son. A decision had also been taken to interdict the North Vietnamese rail system south of the 20th Parallel. On 3 April a strike was made against the giant Ham Rong (Dragon's Jaw) road and rail bridge over the Song Ma River three miles north of Thanh Hoa, the capital of Annam Province, in North Vietnam's bloody 'Iron Triangle' (Haiphong, Hanoi and Thanh Hoa). The 540ft by 56ft Chinese-engineered bridge, which stood fifty feet above the river, was a replacement for the original French-built bridge destroyed by the Viet Minh in 1945, blown up by simply loading two locomotives with explosives and

Above: F4D-1 Skyray of VFAW-3. This delta-winged jet, or 'Ford' as it was fondly dubbed, was another in a long line of fifties fighters which suffered from protracted engine development, and it was five years before the advanced-design, short-range interceptor entered squadron service, with VC-3 on 16 April 1956. Later, as VF(AW)-3, the squadron became the top squadron assigned to the USAF Air Defense Command (ADC). (*Douglas*)

Below: The North American A-5A (A3J-1) Vigilante supersonic bomber's first full squadron deployment was with VAH-7 on board the nuclear carrier *Enterprise*'s first cruise in August 1962. *Enterprise* (CVN-65) was the world's second nuclear-powered surface warship and was commissioned in November 1961. A Vigilante could carry a 3,020lb Mk 27 nuclear store which was ejected rearwards from an internal linear bay, and an ASB-12 bombing-navigation system allowed all-weather attacks on enemy seaports. All heavy-attack squadrons were redesignated RVAH for reconnaissance missions in 1964, all A-5As and Bs being converted to RA-5C configurations. Eighteen RA-5Cs were confirmed lost in combat in Vietnam. (*USN*)

running them together in the middle of the bridge.

Shortly after noon on 3 April, USAF and USN aircraft of 'Rolling Thunder', Mission 9-Alpha, climbed into south-east Asian skies for the bridge at Thanh Hoa. Lt-Cdr Raymond A. Vohden was north of the Dragon when his A-4C Skyhawk was shot down. Vohden was captured and held in various North Vietnamese prison camps until his release in February 1973. An F-8 Crusader was damaged when four F-8Es tried to bomb the bridge and were attacked by MiG-17s. (A USAF RF-101 was hit and went down some seventy-five miles south-west of the target area. From April to September 1965, nineteen more pilots were shot down in the general vicinity of the Dragon, including many who were captured and released.) When the smoke cleared,

observer aircraft found that the two steel through-truss spans which rested in the centre on a massive reinforced concrete pier sixteen feet in diameter were still standing. Numerous hits from the thirty-two Bullpups and ten dozen 750lb bombs aimed at it had charred the structure, yet it showed no signs of going down.

Nearly 700 sorties were flown against the bridge at a cost of 104 crewmen shot down over an area seventy-five square miles around the Dragon. In March 1967 the Navy attacked the charmed bridge with new 'Walleye' missiles but failed to knock out the structure despite three direct hits. The spans were finally brought down on 13 May 1972 by laser-guided 'smart' bombs dropped by F-4Ds of the 8th TFW. Unfortunately, by then the Communists had

---

Below: Vought F-8J Crusader of VF-211 'Fighting Checkmates'. Until the appearance of the F-14A Tomcat in 1973, the single-seat Crusader was the 'last of the gunfighters', probably the finest pure fighter of the jet age, and the Navy's first aircraft capable of more than 1,000 mph. It was also the first variable-incidence (to eliminate an exaggerated nose-up tendency during landing) jet fighter in the world. VF-32 'Swordsmen' were the first squadron to receive the F8U-1 (F-8A), in March 1957. When war broke out in south-east Asia in 1964, F-8Es were the first aircraft to fire their guns in anger when, on 2 August, four Crusaders from the *Ticonderoga*, which at the time were conducting practice firing runs near the carrier, and led by Cdr James B. Stockdale, attacked North Vietnamese PT boats with 20mm cannon and five-inch (127mm) Zuni rockets. Crusaders were in action throughout the Vietnam War, and they remained in front-line service until early in 1976, when the F-8J was retired. (*USN*)

Above: Among the first aircraft from Task Force 77 into action in south-east Asia was the Douglas A-4 Skyhawk. Affectionately known to its pilots as 'Scooter' because of the way it scooted like a balsa plane off the steam catapult, 'Heinemann's Hot Rod' (after the Douglas chief engineer) became one of the most successful attack aircraft in fleet service, December 1962 to 1976. During the 1960s, when the USN usually operated fifteen attack carriers, normally two squadrons in each Carrier Air Wing (CAW) were equipped with Skyhawks (which served alongside one squadron of A-1H Skyraiders). On 4 August 1964, sixty-four aircraft, including fifteen A-4Cs from CVW-14 onboard *Constellation* (CVA-64) and sixteen A-4Es from VA-55 'War Horses' and VA-56 'Champions' of CVW-5 onboard *Ticonderoga*, flew the first retaliatory strikes against North Vietnam, attacking communist naval vessels about seventy miles off the enemy coast. In this photo, on 28 October 1965, an A-4E of VA-23 fires off a salvo of three-inch rockets against Viet Cong positions. (*USN*)

built several other back-up routes around the bridge and the flow of supplies across the Ma River was not seriously affected.

Meanwhile, in April 1965, the war in south-east Asia saw the first intervention by Chinese jets. Two months later, on 17 June, two VF-21 'Freelancers' F-4Bs from *Midway* scored the first MiG kills of the war when they attacked four MiG-17s south of Hanoi and brought down two with radar-guided AIM-7 Sparrow missiles. Cdr Louis C. Page and his radar intercept officer, Lt John C. Smith, together with Lt Jack D. Batson and Lt-Cdr R. B. Doremus, scored the victories, and they were each awarded the Silver Star. Three days later, on 20 June, a third MiG-17 was shot down by Lt Clinton B. Johnson of VA-25 from *Midway*, flying a propeller-driven A-1 Skyraider.

On 12 June 1966 Cdr Hal Marr, CO of VF-211 'Flying Checkmates', equipped with F-8Es aboard the *Hancock*, became the first Crusader pilot to shoot down a MiG when he destroyed a MiG-17 with his second Sidewinder missile at an altitude of only fifty feet. Marr was also credited with a probable after blasting more MiGs with his 20mm cannon. Nine days later, on 21 June, Marr's wingman, Lt(jg) Philip V. Vampatella, shot down another MiG-17 while covering a rescue attempt to bring home an RF-8 pilot shot down earlier.

On 9 October an F-8E pilot, Cdr Dick Bellinger, CO of VF-162 from the USS *Oriskany*, became the first Navy pilot to destroy a MiG-21 when he obliterated one of the enemy fighters with heat-seeking missiles during an escort mission for A-4s from the USS *Intrepid*. But 1966 was a bad year for the US Air Force. Altogether, 379 aircraft were lost, thirty-four of them victims of SA-2 SAM missiles. Some 126 F-105 Thunderchiefs and forty-two F-4s were lost in combat. Something had to be done to drive the MiGs from the skies over North Vietnam.

Phantoms and MiGs met each other in the sky over Vietnam on many occasions throughout the first half of 1967, and American crews also continued to run the gauntlet of SAM missiles and ground fire. On 24 March Lt-Cdr John 'Buzz' Ellison, pilot of an A-6A Intruder in VA-85 'Black Falcons', on board *Kitty Hawk*, was lost, along with his bombadier/navigator, Lt(jg) James Plowman, during a strike force SAM suppression mission against Bac Giang Thermal Power Plant in North Vietnam. The target was defended by SAM sites, light, medium and heavy AA batteries, automatic weapons and small-arms. After the 'bombs away' call, the airborne combat information officer tracked Ellison's aircraft about eleven miles north of the planned track. Radar indications disappeared in the vicinity of Ha Bac Province in northern Vietnam near the border with China. Although Ellison had radio contact with rescuers, he and Plowman were not rescued.

During April–July 1967 the Navy accounted for another dozen enemy aircraft. By the end of the year twenty F-4s and F-105s had been shot down by the MiGs, and a further twenty aircraft by SAMs. One of the worst days occurred on 21 August 1967, when three A-6A Intruders from a four-plane strike force belonging to VA-196 'Main Battery' aboard the *Constellation* were shot down during a raid on the Duc Noi rail yards four miles north of Hanoi. The

Below: Vietnam was the target in September 1965 for these McDonnell F-4B Phantom IIs of VF-41 'Black Aces', VF-84 'Jolly Rogers', and A-4E Skyhawks of VA-86 'Sidewinders' and VA-72 'Blue Hawks', on board *Independence* (CVA-43). Capable of Mach 2.2, the Phantom II resulted from a requirement for a two-seat, twin-engine shipboard fighter, originally ordered in 1954 as a single-seat AH-1 attack aircraft. Probably the most famous of all the aircraft to emerge from the post-Korea era, the world's first truly multi-role supersonic combat aircraft flew on 27 May 1958, and fleet deliveries began on 8 July 1961, when VF-74's 'Bedevillers' at NAS Oceana, Virginia began receiving F-4Bs. Phantoms first saw action in south-east Asia when F-4Bs of CVW-14 on board *Constellation* escorted the first Navy strike, 4 August 1964. The Phantom's arrival in theatre was very opportune, because, although at that time the NVAF had no fighters (they first appeared on 3 April 1965), by the end of the year thirty-four MiG-17s were available, and by June 1965 this number had increased to seventy. By the end of 1965 the NVAF also had supersonic MiG-21s in its inventory. Carrier fighters were first engaged in air-to-air combat on 9 April 1965, when F-4Bs of VF-96 'Fighting Falcons' from the *Ranger* (CV-61) dog-fought with MiG-17s near Hainan. One enemy jet was claimed as 'probably' destroyed, but one Phantom failed to return. Two months later, on 17 June, VF-21 'Freelancers' F-4Bs destroyed the first confirmed MiG victories of the war. (*Douglas*)

Intruders' route from the coast-in point had been uneventful with the exception of some large weather cells building up. Further along their route they received indications of launched SAM missiles and observed bursting 85mm AA fire. Cdr William M. Hardman, the strike leader, and his back-seater, Capt. Leo T. Profilet, were hit in the target area. Both men ejected safely and were captured. The other three Intruders began their egress from the target. Lt-Cdr 'J' Forrest G. Trembley and Dain V. Scott ejected when a SAM detonated between two of the

Intruders. Cdr Jimmy L. Buckley and Lt-Cdr Flynn went down over the Chinese border. Buckley was killed in the shoot-down. Flynn, Hardman and Profilet were held prisoner in China until they were repatriated in March 1973.

On 24 October 1967 Radio Hanoi announced that in the afternoon eight US warplanes had been shot down and that a number of pilots had been captured. Two of the losses were F-4B Phantoms of VF-151 crewed by pilot Cdr Charles R. Gillespie and his back-seater, Lt(jg) Richard Clark, and Earl Lewis

Below: Pressure builds and steam arises on the waist cat on board *Independence* as F-4B '211' BuNo151478 of VF-84 'Jolly Rogers', armed with two AIM-7 Sparrow missiles, is readied for launching on signal from the catapult officer, kneeling at right. The launch weight of the aircraft would be chalked on the black rectangle panel immediately behind the nose radome containing the APQ-72 radar, and undernose IR seeker. For catapult operation Phantoms used a 'bridle' which pulled the aircraft from two strong forgings under the roots of the wings. The bridle was looped over the shuttle and its rear hooks attached to catapult towhooks secured to the Phantom. The shuttle was then eased forward to take up the slack while the Phantom's nose-gear was extended to its full height to jack the aircraft to take-off attitude. Though it cost many hundreds of dollars, it was used only once as it went into the sea at the same time as the Phantom lifted into the sky. (*McDonnell Douglas*)

and Robert Frishmann, from the *Coral Sea*, which were brought down by SAM missiles during a strike on the Hanoi, Haiphong and Vinh Phuc region of North Vietnam. Gillespie, Lewis and Frishmann ejected safely and were captured by the Vietnamese. Frishmann was released in August 1969 and Gillespie and Lewis were both freed from Hanoi on 14 March 1973. On 19 November two more VF-151 F-4Bs, crewed by Lt(jg) James E. Teague and his back-seater, Lt(jg) Theodore G. Stier, and Lt-Cdr Claude D. Clower and Lt(jg) Walter O. Estes, were hit by MiGs over the target at Haiphong. After he was hit, Teague's jet was intact except for small fires burning around the radome and air conditioning, and he began an immediate course change towards the coast. In 1973 Stier and Clower were among 591 Americans released in Operation 'Homecoming' from prisons in and around Hanoi, but in late September 1970 the remains of Teague and Estes were returned by the Vietnamese to US control.

Early in 1968 President Johnson forbade all strikes further than the 19th Parallel, and on 1 November he ordered a halt to all bombing of North Vietnam. This policy was confirmed by the next incoming President, Richard E. Nixon, in January 1969, and the ban on bombing of the North remained in force until May 1972, when the North Vietnamese offensive prompted Nixon to authorise a resumption. 'Linebacker I', as it was called, began with raids against road and rail systems, to prevent supplies reaching the Communists operating in South Vietnam. On 8 May A-6 Intruders sowed minefields in Haiphong, Hon Gai and Cam Pha in the north, and in five ports in the south. At this time the North Vietnamese had one of the best air defence systems in the world, with excellent radar integration of SA-2 SAMs, MiGs and AAA. Losses, though, were kept to within acceptable limits.

The period 10 May to 15 October produced all four American aces (three USAF and one USN) of the Vietnam War. On 10 May, two Navy fliers – Lt Randy 'Duke' Cunningham, pilot of a VF-96 F-4J Phantom, and Lt(jg) William Driscoll, his RIO – operating from the *Constellation* became the first American aircrew to qualify as aces solely as a result of action in Vietnam. Cunningham and Driscoll had

Below: Douglas A-1H/Js (AD-6/AD-7) Skyraiders of VA-52 'Knight Riders' and VA-145 'Swordsmen' were among those aircraft which flew the first retaliatory strikes against North Vietnam, 4 and 5 August 1964. A veteran of the Korean War, fourteen years earlier, the 'Spad', as it was now known, still had much to offer in the war in south-east Asia (a couple even shot down two MiG-17 jets during the conflict). A dozen squadrons were still in service aboard the fast attack carriers, the same number as at the start of the Korean War. Skyraiders flew all manner of attack missions, starting with a strike against the Vinh oil complex on 5 August, when Lt(jg) Richard C. Sather, from CVW-14 on board *Constellation*, became the first naval aviator to be killed in Vietnam. VA-25 'Fist of the Fleet' on board *Coral Sea* was the last Navy squadron equipped with 'Spads' and flew its final combat sorties on 20 February 1968, before retiring its Skyraiders on 10 April. The 'Spad' was the last aircraft to fly from a carrier that did not need the aid of a steam catapult to become airborne. These Skyraiders pictured on the flight deck of the *Hancock* are using fourteen of the fifteen underwing weapons points available for A-1H bombing raids. With centreline fuel tanks, the aircraft could remain airborne for twelve hours and still carry a weapon load of 8,000lb. (*McDonnell Douglas*)

Right: With everything down, F-4B BuNo151492 of VF-84 'Jolly Rogers' prepares to land on board *Independence*. Once fed into the landing approach pattern, concentration is at a peak. During the approach the LSO (Landing Signals Officer), himself a veteran pilot, will talk the pilot down. Attitude, height, rate of descent, engine power and line-up with the deck, all have to be exactly right. The pilot will not be looking at the deck; he will be keeping his eyes on the bright amber 'meatball' on the deck landing sight to the left of the landing area, and he must line up exactly with the green lights each side of the meatball. (*McDonnell Douglas*)

shot down their first MiG on 19 January when the second of two Sidewinders fired blew the tail off a MiG-21. It was the 112th MiG brought down in the war and the tenth to fall to a Navy fighter. Cunningham and Driscoll scored their second kill on 8 May when they downed a MiG-17 with another Sidewinder.

On the 10 May strike (the second that day) VF-96 formed part of a large attack force given the railway yards at Hai Duong, situated between Hanoi and Haiphong. In all, seven F-4J Phantoms, each carrying 2,000lb of Rockeye cluster bombs for flak suppression duties, were launched from the *Constellation*. Their job was to nullify the flak guns while the A-6 Intruders, helped by A-7s armed with anti-radar Shrike missiles to take out the SAM sites, bombed the rail yards. Flak suppression was abandoned, however, when, before the target was reached, the force was intercepted by an estimated twenty-two MiGs. The F-4s dropped their bomb loads on a target of opportunity and climbed in hot pursuit before the enemy fighters could get among the A-6s and A-7s. Lt Matthew J. Connelly III and

Below: Cat shots! F-4B BuNo150491 of VF-41 'Black Aces' is catapulted from the waist deck of the *Independence*, while a brace of A-4 Skyhawks of VA-86 'Sidewinders' and a VA-72 'Blue Hawks' A-4E prepare to launch from the bow cats. The steam catapult develops such brutal thrust that a loaded Phantom could be flung off at full flying speed in just two and a half seconds in a run of 200 feet. Phantoms were noted for their smoky J79 engines. (*Douglas*)

Above: Back from Vietnam an F-4B of VF-84 'Jolly Rogers' races in at a steady 150mph and slams onto the deck of the *Independence* after catching the arresting wire. Once the LSO has given the order 'Clear Deck', the Phantom is taxied away to rearm and refuel, or is struck down below for heavy maintenance in the vast three-and-a-half acre underground hangar deck, about enough space for half a carrier Wing.
(*McDonnell Douglas*)

Below: Although replaced aboard the larger and more modern carriers by E-2A AEW aircraft, the Grumman E-1B Tracer – these are from VAW-111 on board the *Ticonderoga* – provided airborne early warning over the Gulf of Tonkin throughout the Vietnam War. A development of the successful C-1A Trader COD and TF/S-2F Tracker ASW designs, E-1Bs were nicknamed 'Willy Fudds' or the 'Stoof With A Roof' (the S-2F was known as the 'Stoof', while the US2B COD version was referred to as the 'Used to Be'). Traders shuttled personnel, mail and urgently needed supplies from shore bases to carriers, while the S-2 provided invaluable anti-submarine cover for CTF-77 when intervention by Chinese submarines became a possibility. (*USN*)

Above: Turboprop-powered Grumman E-2A Hawkeye of VAW-11 Detachment C about to land on the USS *Kitty Hawk* in 1966. Once airborne the twenty-four-foot dome rotating at 6rpm maintained a radar watch for attacking MiGs and plotted their course, altitude, range and speed. Hawkeyes also directed air strikes to targets whose coordinates were known.
(*Grumman*)

his RIO, Lt Thomas J. Blonski, destroyed two MiG-17s, and two more were destroyed by other VF-96 pilots.

Two MiG-17s latched onto Cunningham and Driscoll's wingman 1,000 feet behind. Just as Cunningham turned the F-4 around the enemy pilot made the fatal mistake of momentarily exposing his underside in a vertical climb. Cunningham fired off a Sidewinder and the MiG-17 exploded. Cunningham turned away and tried to lure another MiG into his wingman's line of sight, but the F-4 pilot had his hands full with other MiGs and Cunningham was forced to disengage. Scanning the sky Cunningham and Driscoll spotted another F-4 with two MiGs on its tail, and another off to the right. Cunningham picked out the nearest MiG-17 and let him have it with another Sidewinder. The enemy jet exploded and the pilot ejected. This action brought four MiG-21s down onto the double MiG killers, and the outnumbered Phantom crew knew it was time to head for the open sea and home. Nearing the coast Cunningham spotted a MiG-17 and, needing just one more for ace status, he decided to try to shoot it down.

The two Americans tacked onto the MiG and a vicious, twisting dog-fight ensued. Cunningham realised that this was no ordinary MiG pilot. (His adversary was Col Toon, the top-scoring NVNAF fighter pilot.) Neither side could gain the initiative and, finally, Toon broke off, probably low on fuel, and headed for home. The Phantom crew gained their first advantage. Now above and behind him they seized the opportunity to fire their one remaining Sidewinder at the retreating MiG. The heat-seeking missile locked on to the enemy's tailpipe and blew the jet to pieces. Cunningham had always said he would never be hit by a SAM. But now, as he turned for home near Haiphong, his F-4 was hit by one of the long telegraph pole-shaped missiles. It failed, however, to bring down the jet. Cunningham managed to fly the badly damaged Phantom back to the *Constellation*, where at 10,000 feet the two men ejected into the sea. They were picked up by a CH-46 helicopter from the *Okinawa* and returned safely to a hero's welcome aboard their own carrier.

Unrestricted use of air warfare finally forced the North's hand. During 18–26 December 1972,

Above: Off Vietnam in 1966, two F-4Bs of VF-114 'Aardvarks' wait behind raised steel walls (jet blast deflectors (JBDs) which rise and fall to protect planes from jet blast), while an F-4G and an F-4B of VF-213 'Black Lions' prepare for launching from *Kitty Hawk*. For approximately two months in 1966, Carrier Air Wing camouflage trials embarked on *Kitty Hawk* and *Constellation* used standard USAF camouflage greens experimentally to reduce losses from ground fire over Vietnam, but the results did not warrant a general change.
(*McDonnell Douglas*)

Below: F-4B Phantom of VF-114 'Aardvarks' ready for catapulting from the deck of the *Kitty Hawk* in April 1966. Twelve Navy F-4Bs were modified into 'G' models by incorporation of a two-day digital data link and an approach power compensation system, both standard in the later F-4J.
(*McDonnell Douglas*)

Above: An F-8E Crusader of VF-162 returns to the USS *Oriskany* (CVA-34) following a strike against the Viet Cong in September 1966. On 9 October Cdr Richard Bellinger, CO of VF-162, and a veteran of World War Two and Korea, gained the Navy's first MiG-21 kill. He assumed command of Air Wing 16 after the CO and forty-three others (twenty-four of them aviators) were killed aboard the *Oriskany* on 26 October when a fire erupted and rapidly spread below decks after a sailor accidentally ignited a magnesium flare, panicked, and then threw it into a storage locker which contained between 600 and 700 more flares. Crewmen bravely moved aircraft and over 300 bombs out of the inferno and threw them overboard. The carrier was out of action for eight months.
(*USN*)

Below: Flight deck crewmen of Early Warning Squadron 33 (VAW-33) make last-minute checks on an EA-1F ECM Skyraider during flight operations aboard the anti-submarine warfare support aircraft carrier USS *Intrepid* (CVS-11) at 'Yankee Station' in the Gulf of Tonkin, 18 September 1967, the last combat mission for a Skyraider in Vietnam.
(*USN*)

Above: This badly damaged VA-212 'Rampant Raiders' A-4E Skyhawk piloted by Lt(jg) Alan R. Crebo tried to land on the deck of the USS *Bon Homme Richard* (CVA-31) after AAA fire during an attack over North Vietnam knocked off the rudder and started a fire at the wing root, 25 April 1967. His wingman, Lt Graham, took this photo when Crebo tried to lower his landing gear. When only the nose wheel and tailhook would come down, a deck landing was out of the question, so Crebo had to eject near the carrier, and he was picked up by helicopter.
(*USN*)

'Linebacker II' operations – all-out, intensive aerial bombardment of industry, communications, ports, supply depots and airfields in the Hanoi and Haiphong areas by the USAF, USN and USMC – were among the most effective of the war. Pilots who flew the missions claimed that the North Vietnamese had 'nothing left to shoot at us as we flew over. It was like flying over New York City.' When the

Communists indicated their desire for a peace settlement on 30 December, the bombing above the 20th Parallel was halted, although missions below the 20th Parallel continued for the first half of January 1973. A peace agreement was signed in Paris on 23 January 1973 and all air operations ceased four days later.

Vietnam cost the Americans 58,022 dead and brought the USA worldwide condemnation for its role in south-east Asia. The USAF and USN could at least draw some solace from the fact that their final intensive campaign had persuaded Hanoi to seek an end to the war and conclude a peace treaty. Although all US ground forces were withdrawn from South Vietnam, air raids into neighbouring Cambodia and Laos continued until August 1973. Both countries then fell to the Communists and the North turned its attentions to the final take-over of South Vietnam. Inevitably, the South, now without US military support, collapsed under the full might of the Communists' spring offensive. On 12 April 1975 the American Embassy in Saigon was evacuated and 287 staff were flown to carriers offshore. On 29 April 900 Americans were airlifted by the Navy to five carriers. Next day Saigon was in Communist hands and the South was under the control of North Vietnam.

Below: F-4B BuNo153011 Phantom of VF-213 'Black Lions' from *Kitty Hawk* dropping Mk 82 Slick 500lb General Purpose bombs on a target in North Vietnam on 23 January 1968. In a throwback to the daylight heavy bomber missions in World War Two, Phantoms flew on bombing strikes in south-east Asia with a lead ship (because the F-4 was not equipped for accurate level bomb delivery), which signalled when to release the bomb load. (*USN*)

Above: A-6A Intruder of VA-85 'Black Falcons' on board the USS *Kitty Hawk* (CVA-63) in the South China Sea. VA-75 'Sunday Punchers', the first operational squadron, began Intruder combat sorties on 1 July 1965 from *Independence* (CAV-62), with attacks against North Vietnam. By 1968, A-6A medium-attack squadrons had replaced all A-1 Skyraiders on carriers. (*Grumman*)

Below: F4-B Phantoms of VF-151 and VF-51 'Screaming Eagles', A-3 Skywarriors, A-6 Intruders and A-4 Skyhawk aircraft aboard the USS *Coral Sea* (CVA-43) in 1969. Altogether, seventeen attack carriers (ten from the Pacific Fleet and seven from the Atlantic Fleet) were used in operations during the Vietnam War. *Hancock* established the record for the number of cruises but *Coral Sea* spent the most days on the line, with 873 days in seven cruises. (*Group Capt. Dave Roome*)

Above: Vought F-8 Crusader of VF-162 on the port cat of USS *Ticonderoga* (CVA-14) in the Gulf of Tonkin in July 1969. Note the comic character Snoopy riding a Sidewinder missile on top of the fin.
(*Bob Gaines*)

Below: A-3D2 BuNo142403 Skywarrior attack aircraft from CWV-9 comes in for recovery aboard the attack carrier USS *America* (CVA-66). Carriers operating in support of the ground battle steamed on 'Dixie Station' in the South China Sea, and those taking part in the war against the North operated from 'Yankee Station' in the Gulf of Tonkin.
(*USN*)

Below: An A-4E Skyhawk of VA-164 'Ghost Riders' from the USS *Oriskany* takes on fuel from a Douglas (A3D-2) KA-3B air refuelling tanker. Although A-3D Skywarriors of VAH squadrons flew some bombing strikes in 1965–6, it was their role as a Navy tanking aircraft from 1967 onwards which realised the 'Whale's' true potential in the Vietnam War. Ninety A-3Bs were modified as KA-3B aerial tankers or EKA-3B tanker/ECM support aircraft, 1967–9. BuNo138974 later served as *Luck of the Irish* in VAH-10, CVW-21, on board the *Hancock*. Some 'Whales' were still in service with VQ-1 and VQ-2 in 1979.
(*McDonnell Douglas*)

Above: A-6A Intruder of VA-165 'Boomers' from CVW-9 on board the attack carrier USS *Constellation* over North Vietnam in 1971. (*Grumman*)

Above: An RA-5C Vigilante of Reconnaissance Attack Squadron 11 (RVAH-11) comes in to to make an arrested landing on the flight deck of *Constellation* in the South China Sea off the coast of South Vietnam, 25 April 1972.

The Vigilante landed fastest of all carrier-based aircraft, at 165 knots.
(*USN*)

Above: Pilots, and Pirate. An A-7E of VA-147 'Argonauts' and an A-6A Intruder of VA-165 'Boomers' in flight during a combat mission in 1972. Both squadrons were part of Attack Carrier Wing Nine (CVW-9) assigned to *Constellation*. VA-147 was established on 1 February 1967 and was the first fleet squadron to operate the A-7A Corsair II, or 'SLUF' as it was known ('Short Little Ugly Fella', although in some circles the acronym is slightly different!). SLUFs were first deployed to Vietnam on the carrier *Ranger* in December 1967. (*USN*)

Below: A-7E Corsair II of Attack Squadron 146 (VA-146) 'Blue Diamonds', ready for launching from the flight deck of the *Constellation* sailing in the Gulf of Tonkin, 25 April 1972, for a strike over Vietnam. A Corsair II could deliver 15,000lb of bombs on target regardless of weather, thanks to its state-of-the-art continuous solution navigation and weapons systems. (*USN*)

CHAPTER 5

OLD AND BOLD:
Restoration, Racing and
Regeneration

Who would have believed, in the aftermath of World War Two, that unwanted military aircraft, sold for surplus at knock-down prices, would one day command six-figure prices? They call them 'ghosts', they call them 'warbirds'. The latter term is now used to describe not just a fighter or bomber with a combat history, but also advanced military trainers and, ultimately, any propeller-driven or jet-powered aircraft that served in the military. Individuals and organisations have turned it into a million-dollar industry which shows little sign of waning in popularity.

Although the numbers of warbirds surviving around the world are but a small proportion of the vast numbers built in production, and flyable examples even smaller, by the late 1990s the world population of warbirds had reached almost 2,500, and about twenty-five per cent of these were flyable. Old favourites like the Mustang lead the way of course, but gaining popularity are the former Navy fighters like the Grumman series of Second World

War and post-war fighters, and the F4U/FG-1D Corsair, of which thirty-one are flyable from the eighty-nine that survive. Nineteen of the surviving forty-four F4F/FM-2 Wildcats, of which 7,905 were built, are flyable. Only eight F6F Hellcats of the twenty-six that still exist (12,275 were built) are flyable. Of the 364 F7F Tigercats built, only six of the dozen that exist are still in flying condition. Some 1,263 F8F Bearcats were built, but just ten are in flying condition out of the twenty-nine that are extant.

Many of these powerful Navy fighters take part in the Reno air races in Nevada, which are held every September. Bearcats are very popular in unlimited racing, particularly at Reno. On 16 August 1969 Lockheed test pilot Darryl Greenmayer in his much modified F8F-2 Bearcat, *Conquest II*, broke the thirty-year-old piston-engine world air speed record with a speed of 483.041mph. (The 545mph set by a Soviet Tu-114 turboprop transport in April 1960 was not officially recognised.) *Conquest II*, which began life as

---

Below: By May 1949 some sixty F8F-2P photo-reconnaissance fighters fitted with just two 20mm wing guns were built. It was not until late 1952 that the last F8F-2P squadron gave up its Bearcats. F8F-2P BuNo121608 (N7700A) was used for Grumman company use. It is flown here by Roger W. Kahn,

head of Grumman's Field Service Dept. In 1960 this aircraft was sold to J. W. 'Bill' Fornorf of Cornell Labs of Houma, Los Angeles, and re-licensed N7700C. Fornorf was killed flying N7700C at NAS Quonset Point, Rhode Island on 5 June 1971. (*Grumman*)

Bu121646, became N7699C when it was bought by Antelope Valley Aerial Surveys of Palmdale, California in 1959. It was acquired by Greenmayer in 1961 and re-registered N1111L. The aircraft is now displayed at the National Air and Space Museum (Paul Garber facility) at Silver Hill, just outside Washington DC. *Conquest II*'s record held until 21 August 1989, when another Bearcat, F8F-2 N777L *Able Cat* ('Rare Bear'), owned by Lyle T. Shelton, set a new world record for a piston-engined aircraft with a speed of 528 mph. It was especially gratifying because N777L (Bu122629) had been wrecked in a crash at Valparaiso, Indiana in 1962 and did not fly again until September 1969, after being rebuilt by Shelton and fitted with a Wright R-3350 engine.

The majority of Navy warbirds like these exist in America and Britain, in museums and as part of huge collections. In the mid-1950s a small band of cropduster pilots in the lower Rio Grande Valley of Texas rescued F8F-2 BuNo121614, one of many Bearcats deteriorating in the hot Arizona sun at NAS Litchfield, where a few years earlier surplus Bearcats had been put out to graze by the Navy. One of the ex-service pilots had bought a war-surplus P-40 in 1951, and in 1957 the Valley flyers acquired a 'surplus' P-51 Mustang. In 1958, these aircraft, including the Bearcat, now registered N7957C, and the men who bought her helped form a loosely defined 'club', which duly became the Confederate Air Force. By 1970 the organisation, which has since spawned many similar gatherings throughout the world, had established itself at Harlingen, Texas, and it has developed into the world's finest and most complete collection of flyable World War Two combat aircraft. Eventually, the CAF went on to own three Bearcats. F8F-2, BuNo122619, which was obtained in 1966 and sold in 1972, is currently on display at the EAA Museum at Oshkosh as N14WB. N7957C was written off in an accident in May 1974.

Above and below: Kermit Weeks in his Grumman FM-2 Wildcat BuNo86741 (N222FM) in the colours of VC-12 photographed over his Fantasy of Flight Museum in Polk County, Florida, by Ed Toth. Eastern Aircraft, a division of General Motors, was awarded a contract for 1,800 Wildcats on 18 April 1942. Production of the FM-1 and Martlet V aircraft began at their Linden, New Jersey plant, one of five on the east coast. Production really got under way in 1943 when 1,437 FM-1, Wright R-1820-56 Cyclone-powered FM-2, and Martlet V aircraft were built by Eastern. (*Ed Toth*)

The third Bearcat, F8F-2P BuNo122674 N7825C, was donated to the CAF on 8 February 1972.

Warbirds participate each year at the Confederate Air Force show, now held at Midland, Texas, every October, and on the US air show circuit at venues like Oshkosh, Wisconsin, home of the Experimental Aircraft Association; Sun 'N' Fun, Lakeland; at TICO, Florida; and the Wings of Eagles show in New York State. In Europe they grace shows like Flying Legends at Duxford every July, and at La Ferte Alais

Above and left: PV-2 Harpoon BuNo37396 (N7265C) *Hot Stuff*, photographed by Ed Toth. PV-1 Venturas were credited with sinking four U-boats in the Atlantic in 1943. In the Pacific, the Ventura equipped FAW-4. On 30 June, Lockheed-Vega received an order for 500 PV-2 Harpoons, a much bigger development of the PV-1, with greater wing area, longer range, ten machine-guns, new tail and the ability to carry up to ten .5-inch rockets and 4,000lb of bombs or torpedoes. Service deliveries began in March 1944. PV-2s equipped fourteen Navy squadrons and were first used in April 1944 from Attu in bombing and rocket strikes on Japanese positions in the Kuriles. Two other PV-2 squadrons fought in the central Pacific. During the last few months of the Pacific War Harpoons carried out bombing and rocket attacks on the Kuriles, Truk, Wake and others, and patrolled shipping lanes near Guam, Saipan and other American bases. PV-2s remained in Navy service until 1948, although they served with reserve patrol squadrons until the late 1950s. (*Author*)

in France. Gaining popularity, it seems, are non-fighter types like the TBF/TBM Avenger, thirty-seven of which are flyable, and the SBD Dauntless, twenty-five of which survive, although only two are flyable. At the other end of the scale, just one SB2C Helldiver from the eleven that survive is flyable.

Increasingly, more and more warbirds continue to be found, are restored over several years, and put back into airworthy condition, much to the enjoyment of their owners and the aviation-minded

public alike. Of course, the cost is not inconsiderable. It can take the best part of a quarter of a million dollars to restore a fighter from the ground up. Keeping them flying can be as critical. It costs up to $50,000 a year to keep a fighter in the air, and an engine overhaul can run from $40,000 to $70,000, depending on the parts that are needed.

Of all the rare and exotic machines on the market, none can compare with a flyable warbird in pristine condition, and those in shades of Navy blue remain among the most attractive for collectors, users and speculators alike.

Above: PBY-6A Catalina BuNo64072 N7057C, owned and operated by the National Warplane Museum, photographed over Lake Ontario, west of Rochester, in August 1992 by Dick Bagg. Some 3,290 Cats were built, and of the ninety-five that survive, forty are in flying condition. (*Dick Bagg*)

Below: PV-2 Harpoon *Fat Cat Too* belonging to the Combat Aircraft Museum at Lafayette, Louisiana, photographed by the author in flight from Lakeland, Florida in 1994, when it was Reserve Grand Champion (Warbird) at Sun 'N' Fun. The original *Fat Cat* was destroyed in a fire at Conroe, Texas in 1990. Named after the 'fat cats', or top brass, she once ferried around, *Fat Cat Too* was assigned by VPB-139 at Whidbey Island, Washington, and after completion of crew assignment and training was placed in the Duty Roster. Several hours after her departure to Attu in the Aleutians she was ordered to return to base. The aircraft was reassigned to VPB-136 and spent the remainder of the war years on maritime patrol out of Panama, cruising the eastern coast of South America in search of Japanese submarines or surface supply vessels. (*Author*)

Above: F6F-5K BuNo80141 (G-BTCC), which belongs to the Fighter Collection at Duxford, is the only Hellcat flying outside the USA and has a long and chequered history. For four years, 1965–9, 80142 (N80142) was displayed at the USMC Museum at MCAS Quantico, VA before being purchased by Thomas H. Friedkin in California, who re-registered the aircraft as N100TF. After a crash landing in April 1979, the Hellcat passed to the Yankee Air Corps at Chino, CA, who carried out a rebuild during 1985–8 by using the centre-section of BuNo08831. In 1990 the aircraft arrived at Duxford, where it joined Stephen Grey's Fighter Collection, and was subsequently repainted to represent BuNo40467 of VF-6 flown by Lt(jg) Alex Vraciu. (*Author*)

Below: F6F-5N BuNo94204 (N4998V) of the Lone Star Flight Museum at Galveston, Texas, in flight at Oshkosh. This Hellcat was rebuilt at Hayward, California. A total of 1,432 F6F-5Ns was built. (*Author*)

Below: Grumman TBM-3R BuNo53319 (N3966A) Avenger flown by owner Tony Haig-Thomas, on finals during a flying display at Duxford. (*Author*)

Above: Restored TBM-3E BuNo85886 (N9586Z) belonging to the TBF Inc., Tenafly, New Jersey, which flies as SL-401. The last of the TBM-3Es were withdrawn from VS-27 in October, 1954, bringing to an end twelve and a half years of service use. (*Author*)

Above: TBM-3/3U Bu53835 (N3967A) in flight at Ellington Field, Houston, Texas. This Avenger, which belongs to the Skarda Flying Service at Hazen, Arizona, flies as GS-41. A total of 4,661 TBM-3s were manufactured, April 1944 to September 1945. Post-war, many TBMs and TBFs saw action as water-bombers and were used to fight forest fires. (*Author*)

Above: Curtiss SB2C-5 BuNo83589 (N92879) Helldiver of the American Airpower Heritage Flying Museum (Confederate Air Force), Midland, Texas. This aircraft's last military assignment was with VA-103 at NAS Glenview in 1962, and the aircraft joined the CAF at Harlingen in November 1971.

The SB2C-5, which began appearing in February 1945, was the last of the Helldiver series built, a total of 970 being produced with a 2,100hp Cyclone, APS-4 radar, and increased fuel tankage, before production ceased in October 1945. (*Bill Crump/CAF*)

Above: F4U-4 F-AZVJ Corsair on finals at Duxford. (*Author*)

Above: F8F-2P BuNo121714 (N700HL) belonging to the Fighter Collection, and painted in the colours of VF-41 'Red Rippers', pictured on a rain-swept day at Duxford in 1992. By May 1949 some sixty F8F-2P photo-reconnaissance fighters fitted with just two 20mm wing guns were built. It was not until late 1952 that the last F8F-2P squadron gave up its Bearcats. (*Author*)

Below: F8F-2 BuNo121752 (N800H) on finals at Duxford. Formerly N7827C and N2YY, this Bearcat was raced in the USA, 1964–90, as *Tom's Cat*, *Miss Priss*, *Sweet Pea*, *Precious Bear* and, finally, *Bearcat Bill*, until it was acquired by the late Doug Arnold in 1990. The F8F-2 was ordered on 28 June 1946. It was powered by an R-2800-30W variable-speed supercharged engine equipped with water injection and an automatic engine control unit. A twelve-inch extension to the vertical fin improved stability. A 150-gallon droppable fuel tank could be installed on the fuselage bomb rack, and a 100-gallon droppable tank on each wing bomb rack. (*Author*)

Above: AD-4NA (A-1D) BuNo126922 Skyraider of the Fighter Collection on finals at Duxford. This aircraft, which saw operational service in Madagascar and the Gabon, is painted in the livery of the MiG-17 killing aircraft operated by Lt(jg) William T. Patton of VA-176 'Thunderbolts' on board *Intrepid* in October 1966 during the Vietnam War.

The other shooting down of a MiG-17 by a Skyraider occurred on 20 June 1965 when Lt Clinton B. Johnson of VA-25 from *Midway* was credited with the victory. VA-176, flying A-6E Intruder and KA-6D tankers, was disestablished on 1 October 1991. (*Author*)

Below: FG-1D BuNo92399/NX448AG, in the colours of VF-17, in formation with P-51D *Hurry Home Honey* and

P-47D *Big Ass Bird II*, photographed by Tom Smith.

Above: Six Corsairs in formation from Oshkosh in 1994. Nearest aircraft is FG-1D BuNo92468 (N9964Z) '13/USS *Essex*' of the American Airpower Heritage Flying Museum, Midland, Texas. Next is FG-1D BuNo92509 '611' (N3PP) of the Kalamazoo Aviation History Museum. (*Tom Smith*)

Above: F9F-3 BuNo123072 (N72WP) of the Flying Warbirds Foundation, Philadelphia, Pennsylvania, in the livery of VF-112, photographed by Dick Bagg in August 1990 near Geneseo, New York. This Panther was rebuilt by Bill Pryor and Harry Drummond using parts from the hulk of BuNo137180 from the Philadelphia Navy yard.

Below: A pair of Beech T-34As in close formation over Florida. The Mentor was the major primary trainer for the USAF and the USN in the 1950s and led to the USN turboprop-powered T-34C version. (*Author*)

Above: North American T-28B BuNo138356 (NX91AW) in the training colours of VT-27, owned and flown by John Morgan, photographed by Ed Toth. Although built as a basic trainer, 1949–57, and used as such by both the USAF and the Navy, the Trojan proved a powerful COunter-INsurgency (COIN) aircraft in the hands of the French (T-28D Nomad) in Algeria. Starting in 1961, the 'Farm Gate' Detachment (4400th Combat Crew Training Squadron, or 'Jungle Jim', as they were nicknamed; later, 1st Air Commando) at Tan Son Nhut, Vietnam, initially used up to thirteen armed T-28Bs on COIN operations in south-east Asia. Eight were USN models, which, with their 1,425hp R-1820-86 engines, were more powerful than the 800hp Wright used in the Air Force version. Up to 4,000lb of external stores, including gun pods, could be carried by the Trojans. On 26 December 1961 the first USAF bombing mission in south-east Asia was flown by two T-28Bs and two Vietnamese AD-6s against VC facilities north of Saigon. T-28s were used by the 1st ACS at least until April 1964, when two American pilots were killed when their Trojan's wings broke up in the air.

Above: North American T-28C BuNo140581 (N581JS), and T-28B BuNo138130, photographed by Ed Toth. Navy Trojans differed from the USAF models in having their nosewheel steering deleted. The C in the foreground is fitted with an arrester hook for carrier training.

Above: During a strike on Kep airfield on 1 May 1967 Lt-Cdr T. R. 'Ted' Swartz in BuNo148609, a VA-76 A-4C on board USS *Bon Homme Richard*, was firing Zuni rockets at aircraft on the ground when his wingman told him there was a MiG-17 on his tail. Swartz pulled above and behind his pursuer and fired off more Zunis, which brought down the enemy jet. It was the only MiG kill by unguided rockets in the whole of the Vietnam War. This rebuilt A-4B, BuNo142112 (N3E), which was owned by Combat Jets Flying Museum at Houston, Texas, until 1992, when it was acquired by the EAA Aviation Foundation at Oshkosh, Wisconsin, is painted to represent Swartz's original aircraft. (*Author*)

CHAPTER 6
STORM CLOUDS

Not since the Vietnam War had America needed to deploy its vast and impressive Navy in a full-scale war, but in the early 1980s the 6th Fleet in the Mediterranean, in particular, proved a very efficient avenger, and then deterrent, in the fight against international terrorism. An uneasy peace existed between Libya and the United States, and in 1981 Colonel Gadaffi, President of Libya, threw down the gauntlet when he announced that, contrary to all international maritime law, Libyan territorial waters were to be extended to nearly 480km (300 miles), incorporating the Gulf of Sidra.

In response, the nuclear-powered aircraft carrier *Nimitz*, which had left its US east coast home port on 3 August, headed to the Mediterranean with its support vessels to join up with the *Forrestal* (which in 1955 had been the first carrier built to handle jet aircraft) for training exercises which would culminate in a live missile firing in a test zone which would include part of the Gulf of Sidra area. On 18 August the two battle groups were probed on several occasions by sections of Libyan fighters. On 19 August the flashpoint was reached when two Libyan Sukhoi Su-22s attempted to shoot down a pair of F-14As from VF-41 'Black Aces' operating from the *Nimitz*. In less than a minute, Cdr Henry 'Hank' Kleeman and Lt Dave Venlet, and Lt Larry Muczynski and Lt Jim Anderson, destroyed the two 'Fitter-Js' over the Gulf of Sidra with AIM-9L Sidewinder AAMs.

Below: Grumman F-14A Tomcat of the famous VF-14 'Tophatters' on board the USS *John F. Kennedy* (CV-67). The Tomcat was a result of an early 1960s USN requirement for a high-performance fighter to replace the ageing F-4 Phantom. The first of twelve research and development aircraft made its maiden flight on 21 December 1970, and the first production aircraft was delivered to the Navy in June 1972. For two years an evaluation of the type was carried out. When the Tomcat began an eight-month deployment to the Western Pacific with VF-1 and VF-2 on board the 90,000-ton nuclear-powered *Enterprise* (CVN-65) in mid-September 1974, it was the world's first operational air superiority fighter with a variable-sweep wing. VF-14's 'Tophatters' and VF-32's 'Swordsmen' were the first Atlantic fleet units equipped with the Tomcat, and put to sea aboard 'Big John' in June 1975, to take up station with the 6th Fleet in the Mediterranean. (*Author*)

Above: From the early 1980s to the early 1990s, the 6th Fleet was on station during an uneasy peace between Libya and the US. Long-range bombers armed with sea-skimming missiles posed the main threat to Navy vessels and only the Grumman F-14 Tomcat could intercept them before they were in range. On 19 August 1981 F-14As from VF-41 'Black Aces' (pictured) operating from the *Nimitz* shot down two Libyan Sukhoi Su-22s that were approaching the battle group in a hostile manner. (*Author*)

In December 1983 CVW-3 on board the 82,000-ton *John F. Kennedy* (CV-67), the 'Big John' or 'Slack Jack' as it is known, flew combat sorties over Lebanon. In an experiment, the two usual LTV A-7E squadrons were replaced with a second Intruder squadron, and this resulted in VA-75, VA-85 and VA-176 (which had flown combat sorties over Grenada in October 1983) being embarked on board. On 4 December an Intruder of VA-85 was lost during a retaliatory strike against Syrian AAA sites.

Two years later, on 27 December 1985, terrorists attacked the EL-AL check-in counter at airports in Rome and Vienna, killing fourteen people, including an eleven-year-old American girl, and injuring fifty others. The attack was thought to be Libyan-backed. In late January 1986 Gadaffi established his so-called 'line of death' in the Gulf of Sidra from a point just south of Tripoli across to Benghazi, and warned that any American aircraft or surface vessels entering it would be destroyed. America's patience was exhausted, and in February 1986 Operation 'Prairie Fire' was launched to provoke Libya into a direct military confrontation.

Three carrier battle groups crossed the 'line of death', and on 24 March two SA-5 'Gammon' missiles were fired at the 6th Fleet but both missed their targets. Later that day two F-14A Tomcats chased off a pair of MiG-25 'Foxbat-A' interceptors, and tension increased as more missiles were fired at the carrier groups. Two Grumman A-6E Intruders sank a Libyan Nanutchka-class missile patrol boat with AGM-84A Harpoon anti-ship missiles and Rockeye cluster bombs. Vought A-7E Corsairs badly damaged a shore installation with AGM-88A High-Speed Anti-Radiation (HARM) missiles, and further attacks on Libyan targets were carried out by more A-6Es and A-7Es. A total of four Libyan vessels had been destroyed or damaged and one or two SAM sites knocked out.

Regrettably, terrorist action continued on 5 April when a bomb left by a Palestinian terrorist exploded in the La Belle disco in West Berlin, frequented by hundreds of off-duty US personnel. A US Army sergeant and a Turkish woman were killed and 230 people were injured, including seventy-nine US servicemen. The Libyan regime clearly backed the attack. More bomb plots were uncovered by intelligence sources, aimed at US military targets around the world, with ten planned for Berlin alone. Certainly, swift action was needed to deter the terrorists and their Libyan paymasters. In 1986 the decision was taken to bomb terrorist-related targets

Above: A-6E BuNo161659 TRAM (Target Recognition and Attack Multisensor) Intruder ready for launch when it will accelerate from 0 to 160 knots in just four seconds. In March 1986, during the 'Prairie Fire' operation, launched to provoke Libya into a direct military confrontation, two A-6E Intruders sank a Libyan fast-attack craft with AGM84A Harpoon anti-ship missiles and Rockeye cluster bombs. On 14 April 1986 Operation 'El Dorado Canyon', the American bombing of terrorist-related targets in Libya, went ahead. Targets for the fourteen A-6Es from the USS *America* and USS *Coral Sea* in the eastern Mediterranean were the Al Jumahiriya barracks in Benghazi, and Benina airport outside the city. Overall, 'El Dorado Canyon' was a great success. Two days after the attacks post-strike reconnaissance by two SR-71As confirmed that all five targets had been well hit. (*Grumman*)

Below: F-14A Tomcats flew top cover for the attack forces during 'El Dorado Canyon'. No matter how impressive the strike power within the Carrier Air Wing, effective over-the-horizon AEW (Airborne Early Warning) and co-ordination of operations are essential if a strike is to succeed. The Grumman E-2C Hawkeye, or 'Hummer', as the flying radar station is known, with its huge 24ft diameter rotodome housing the General Electric APS96 search radar, has been the airborne 'eyes of the fleet' for well over thirty years, ever since becoming operational with VAW-11 on board *Kitty Hawk* in the Gulf of Tonkin, late in 1965 in fact. (*Author*)

Above: Part of the air component for 'El Dorado Canyon' were six F/A-18A Hornets from the *Coral Sea* which, together with six A-7Es from the USS *America*, blasted the SAM and radar installations with Shrike and HARM air-to-surface missiles at Libyan air defence sites along the coast and in and around Benghazi. The first Hornet prototype had flown on 18 November 1978 and first went to sea in February 1985 with VFA-25 'Fist of the Fleet' and VFA-113 'Singers', part of CVW-14 aboard the *Constellation* (CVA-64). Conceived as a multi-mission aircraft, the Hornet superseded the F-4 Phantom fighter, A-4 Skyhawk and A-7E attack aircraft in USMC and USN squadrons (redesignated VFA (Strike-Fighter)). Following Operation 'El Dorado Canyon', F/A-18C Hornets of VFA-86 'Sidewinders' replaced A-7Es aboard the USS *America*, and these were on board the carrier with the rest of CVW-1 during deployment in the Gulf Crisis, November 1990. (*McDonnell Douglas*)

at Tripoli and Benghazi, using USAF F-111Es based in Britain and carrier-borne aircraft in the eastern Mediterranean. The F-111s were given three targets in the Libyan capital, Tripoli, while attack planes from the USS *America* and USS *Coral Sea* were to carry out strikes against the Al Jumahiriya barracks in Benghazi, and Benina airport outside the city.

Operation 'El Dorado Canyon', as it was code-named, went ahead on 14 April 1986. At 2220 hours the first of eight A-6E Intruders of VA-55 'War Horses' and six F/A-18A Hornets from CVW-13 were launched from the deck of the *Coral Sea*. Starting at 2245 and ending at 2315, six A-6Es of VA-34 'Blue Blasters' and six Vought A-7E Corsair IIs from CVW-1 were catapulted off the deck of the *America*. F-14A Tomcats took off to fly top cover for the attack forces while E-2C Hawkeyes carried out their AEW tasks and KA-6Ds carried out inflight refuelling. EA-6B Prowlers began their ECM jamming of Libyan radars while the A-7Es and F/A-18As on TARCAP (target combat air patrol) blasted the SAM and radar installations with Shrike and AGM-88 HARM air-to-surface missiles at Libyan air defence sites along the coast and in and around Benghazi. The A-6E bombing runs with 500lb and

750lb bombs began at 0001, simultaneously with the USAF strikes on Tripoli. Two days after the attacks post-strike reconnaissance by two SR-71As confirmed that all five targets had been well hit.

During Operation 'Praying Mantis', 18–19 April 1988, A-6Es of VA-95 'Green Lizards' from CVW-11 on board *Enterprise* in the Arabian Gulf sank an Iranian Boghammar speedboat and damaged another with Rockeye cluster bombs. Later, after evading SAMs fired by the Iranian frigate *Sahand*, two VA-95 crews severely damaged *Sahand* with Harpoon missiles and Skipper laser-guided bombs. After taking another Harpoon hit from a US destroyer, *Sahand* almost sank when fires reached her magazines. Later, *Sahand* drew fire from VA-95 after the ship fired a SAM at the Intruders. One A-6E hit *Sahand* with laser-guided bombs, leaving the ship dead in the water; the ship was taken under tow with its stern submerged. In January 1989, two F-14A Tomcats from VF-32 'Swordsmen', working in conjunction with an E-2C Hawkeye, all from CVW-3 on board *Kennedy*, destroyed two Libyan MiG-23 'Floggers' with Sparrow and Sidewinder missiles.

On 2 August 1990 President Saddam Hussein of Iraq massed seven divisions and 2,000 tanks along

Top: An EA-6B, its split wingtip speedbrakes out, prepares to land on board. The Prowler's forward fuselage is stretched to accommodate a second cockpit for two EW operators and the rear fuselage is extended to balance the aircraft. Prowler is the standard USN carrier-borne ECM aircraft and is intended to confuse, and identify, enemy radars, and assist and escort friendly combat aircraft. The EA-6B first flew on 25 May 1968, and delivery of the first production models began in 1971. The new Prowler represented a dramatic improvement over the original EA-6A, which had first flown in 1963. EA-6B Prowlers took part in 'El Dorado Canyon', used to carry out ECM jamming of Libyan radars while the strike force attacked. In the Gulf War, 16 January to 28 February 1991, an EA-6B electronic warfare (EW) squadron was included in each Carrier Air Wing on board the Navy carriers. (*Author*)

Above: 'Cats on the prowl'. Night attack specialists VA-35 'Black Panthers' are the oldest attack squadron in the USN (formed as VB-3 in the 1930s). A-6E BuNo161659 is seen here, part of CVW-17 on board the USS *Saratoga* during the Gulf War. VA-35 lost two Intruders on the first day of the war, one returning to the carrier but damaged beyond economical repair. Over western Iraq in the second week of Operation 'Desert Storm', *Saratoga*'s Air Wing lost an F-14B from VF-103 'Sluggers' during a reconnaissance mission on 21 January, and an F-18C, piloted by Lt-Cdr Michael Speicher, both to SAMs. This was the only occasion a Tomcat was lost during the conflict, pilot Lt Devon Jones being picked up by helicopter and Lt Laurence Slade, his back-seater, being taken prisoner. (*Grumman*)

Above: 'Feline friends'. A heavily armed F-14A Tomcat of VF-41 'Black Aces' with an AIM-54C Phoenix long-range AAM below the fuselage centreline, from the nuclear-powered *Theodore Roosevelt* (CVN-71), photographed on 23 January 1991 by RAF Squadron Leader Mike Rondot from his 41 Squadron Jaguar (XZ358) near Faylaka Island, ten miles east of Kuwait City.

the Iraq–Kuwait border, and they invaded Kuwait in the early morning hours. On 7 August, after Iraq refused to remove its troops from Kuwait, President Bush ordered 'Desert Shield' to begin, sending warplanes and ground forces to Saudi Arabia, saying the country faced the 'imminent threat' of an Iraqi attack. Within thirty-five days the USAF had deployed a fighter force that equalled Iraq's fighter capability in numbers. America's huge carrier battle groups were also placed on full war alert. In August

Below: F-14A from VF-211 'Fighting Checkmates' launching an AIM-54A Phoenix missile. While the Tomcat can carry up to six of these $1 million missiles, because of weight considerations during recovery back aboard a carrier, the F-14 usually carries just two, on the forward stations LAU-93s. Main missile armament comprises four AIM-7E Sparrow MRAAMs partially recessed under the fuselage or four Phoenix mounted below. In addition, four AIM-9L/M Sidewinder SRAAMs, or two Sidewinders plus two Phoenix or two Sparrow, can be carried on two underwing pylons. (*Grumman*)

Above: 'Pussy Galore'. A-6E Intruders of VA-65 'Tigers', part of CVW-8, flying in formation from the USS *Theodore Roosevelt*. During the Gulf War, VA-65 and VA-36 'Road Runners' formed the medium-attack component on board the carrier for Operation 'Desert Storm' (normally carriers only carried one A-6E medium attack). VA-36 lost an A-6E on 2 February when both crew were killed. (*USN via Grumman*)

Below: Primary Flight Control keeps track of flight operations by logging up-to-the-minute data on launches and recoveries on straightforward yet effective large-format displays throughout the carrier. With up to a hundred-plus sorties a day during exercises and in war, accurate and instant information on the location of every aircraft – there are usually nine squadrons aboard – is vital. (*Author*)

1990 the *John F. Kennedy*, with CVW-3 on board, was redeployed back to the Mediterranean. On 4 August *Saratoga* deployed with CVW-17 on board, and in September *Midway*, with CVW-5 on board, left its home port of Yokosuka, Japan, for the Indian Ocean, where it replaced *Independence* (CV-62). *Indy*, with CVW-14 on board, had been the first carrier to 'take station' off the Gulf, and she returned to home port San Diego. On 8 December the *Ranger* sailed from California with CVW-2 on board, and was followed on 28 December by the *America* (CV-66), with CVW-1 on board, and the *Theodore Roosevelt*, with CVW-8 on board. *America* replaced the *Eisenhower* in the Red Sea before war operations commenced. *Roosevelt* arrived just in time to transit from an initial position in the Red Sea to the Gulf station. In the Persian Gulf, *America*, *Midway*, *Ranger* and *Theodore Roosevelt* became what was known as Battle Force Zulu, while

Kennedy with CVW-3 on board (VA-46 'Clansmen' and VA-72 'Blue Hawks' A-7Es were on their last operational deployment before the Corsair II was replaced by F/A-18s) remained in the Red Sea. *America* became the only carrier to operate in both the Persian Gulf and the Red Sea.

Each of these carriers carry up to nine squadrons. These normally include two F-14A fighter, one A-6E medium attack, two F/A-18 light attack squadrons, an S-3A and an SH-3H squadron for ASW, an EA-6B electronic warfare (EW) squadron, and an E-2C AEW squadron. Maritime reconnaissance in the Gulf was carried out by P-3C Orions and carrier-based S-3 Vikings, while tactical air reconnaissance missions were flown from the carriers by TARPs (tactical air reconnaissance pod system)-equipped F-14s (normally three Tomcats in each squadron per carrier).

Efforts to find a peaceful resolution with Iraq

Below: Mighty carriers at flight time are potentially the most dangerous place in the world. They turn into wind and the PRI-FLY (Primary Flight Control), or Air Boss, blares out movement instructions on the Tannoy. He controls the air round the carrier to a height of 5,000 feet and a circumference of five miles. Everything else is controlled from the Combat Centre deep below the bulkheads. On deck a VF-14 'Tophatters' Tomcat taxies by as flight personnel wait patiently. Another F-14A, and an F/A-18C, the next customers, check in behind the raised jet blast deflectors aft of the VAQ-141 'Shadowhawks' EA-6B and VQ-6 'Ravens' ES-3A Shadow. Aviation fuel will mix a heady cocktail with the salty sea air as the JBDs try to disperse the efflux from their dry-thrust turbofans, before falling again to allow through to the cats the two big jets with their afterburners. Then things get *really* hot! (The deck between the launch point and the JBDs has its own internal watercooling system.) It is as if twenty major airshows have been harnessed into one enormous production. (*Author*)

Above: With the Tomcat positioned over the catapult, its gross weight is set on a capacity safety valve by the catapult officer, who chalks the figure on a board and shows it to the pilot. The latter confirms that the figure is correct with a thumbs-up signal and the figure is then passed to the 'shooters' in their revetment immediately in front of the Tomcat, who watch steam pressure build up in below-deck accumulators and ensure that enough pressure is available to handle the weight shown. (Cats are pre-set to a tension value of 4,000lb, although the steam pressure is adjustable according to the type and size of aircraft.) When the steam has risen to the appropriate pressure a light shows on the catapult firing panel and the JBDs rise behind the aircraft. When the deck officer drops to his knee and points to the bow the 'shooters' will signal to the engineers below deck to fire the catapult. Meanwhile, an SPO checks that the nose gear fixed towbar on this 'Black Aces' F-14A has properly engaged the catapult shuttle. A retaining link visible behind the nosewheel holds the aircraft against full thrust and will snap off as the catapult reaches its full working pressure. All four catapults under the deck comprise two 300ft cylinders, each with a metal valve running along its entire length. The shuttle is attached to a piston in each cylinder by a link which opens and closes the valves as it passes. (*Author*)

Above: If the alert state is high prior to a launch, the F-14 crew will remain strapped in their aircraft for anything up to two hours. Seconds before the launch, the catapult officer waits for the pilot to complete his final checks on systems and flight controls before the latter gives him the signal to fire. A carrier is like a rock with just the occasional 'shimmy' as the mighty vessel changes course, or turns into wind for launching to commence. At right is an E-2C Hawkeye of VAW-124 (Carrier Airborne Early Warning Squadron 124). During 'Desert Storm' the 'Bear Aces' operated from the USS *Theodore Roosevelt*. (*Author*)

proved futile. Finally, on 16 January 1991, Operation 'Desert Storm' began, and all-out attacks by land-based strike aircraft in Saudi Arabia and Turkey, and by naval aircraft units and missiles at sea, were made against Saddam Hussein's forces. The war began during the night of 17 January with the launching of fifty-two Tomahawk land-attack cruise missiles from the battleship *Wisconsin*, and other surface ships, against a variety of Iraqi targets. On this date, two pilots, Lt-Cdr Mark Fox and Lt Nick Mongillo from VFA-81 'Sunliners', scored the Navy's only fixed-wing aerial victories of the war, and the first ever kills for the Hornet, when they shot down two Iraqi MiG-21s while en route to a target. This they also successfully bombed before returning to their carrier.

While conventional cruise missile attacks launched from ships hundreds of miles away were an important element of the first phase of the operations, they did not have the long-term impact of sustained naval air operations. 'Desert Storm' had already passed through two distinct phases by the end of the third week in the war with Iraq. Naval air

power, based largely, from mid-February, upon six carrier-based air wings operating in the Arabian Gulf and Red Sea, had accounted for one third of all air sorties, despite adverse flight ranges of typically 450 to 650 miles from the carriers, which required most aircraft to perform at least one aerial refuelling from USAF, and USN KA-6D tanker aircraft each mission, and navigational restrictions imposed by the area of these waters.

Much of the success in 'Desert Storm', and its speedy conclusion, (President George Bush announced a ceasefire in the Gulf War on 28 February) derived from the widespread use of hi-tech laser-, TV- and infra-red-guided bombs and rockets throughout early air operations. The tempo of USN operations was above that flown during the Vietnam War, averaging 125 to 150 sorties per day per carrier (weather permitting). Operations were flown by day and by night, with about half the sorties being strike missions flown by F/A-18, A-7E and A-6E TRAM-equipped attack aircraft. As during the Vietnam operations, one carrier 'on the line' was

Above and below: A VF-41 'Black Aces' pilot selects the full 20,900lb afterburning thrust that is available from the two Pratt & Whitney TF30s, and his F-14A Tomcat goes from zero to 150 knots in 2.2 seconds, and hurtles off the bow of the *Kennedy* at mesmerising speed. At sea level the F-14A can climb at up to 30,000 feet a minute. Some of the early accidents involving Tomcats with TF30 engines arose from compressor stall when applying afterburner during launch. Take-offs from carriers in the later marks of Tomcat with their two General Electric F1210s, rated at 23,100lb afterburning thrusts, can safely be made dry, without afterburner.
(*Author*)

Above: Morning, noon or night, there is no finer sight aboard a carrier than to witness the launch of a combat jet from its flight deck. Both aircraft having left the waist catapults, the Cat/AG Officer beckons forth another pair of aircraft for launching. An aircraft can warm up on one waist catapult while another is launched, and the two widely spaced bow catapults can be used almost simultaneously. (*Author*)

Above: Apart from the helicopter, arrival aboard a carrier at sea is made in a Grumman C-2A or COD (Carrier Onboard Delivery), like '53' of VRC-40 'Rawhides', which is trapped aboard the *John F. Kennedy* in the Mediterranean after a flight from Sigonella, Sicily. The C-2A is a lumbering, benevolent bear of a plane, hardly sleek, but one which surprisingly goes by the name of Greyhound. Passengers sit facing the rear. Those who can see out will notice that even at 4.56 acres and 1,051½ft by 252ft, a carrier and its landing pad below look very small! There are a few stomach-turning moments as the COD passes the carrier at 250 feet, banks sharply to port in a full battle break, and sidles in for a pulsating, exciting few seconds into the landing pattern. Closer, closer – then thump! The tailhook catches one of the carrier's four arrester cables which stops it dead in its tracks with a heart-stopping jolt. (*Author*)

usually engaged in support functions, such as at-sea refuelling or munitions and logistic replenishment, at any given time, with the carrier's flight schedule reduced accordingly.

The technology demonstrated in the Gulf has

Below: The 300ft catapult, hot and steaming and smelling of burning rubber after a launch. (*Author*)

rendered the costly and long-drawn-out battles which were fought in the past largely redundant. NATO forces, however, remain on constant alert, and exercises and scenarios are one way of maintaining operational readiness. The USN is the leading player in joint naval exercises such as 'Dynamic Mix', a NATO-led, joint, multinational, live exercise in the Mediterranean. For 'Dynamic Mix', 22 September to 7 October 1997, America alone provided no fewer than eleven ships with a total of 14,000 US sailors and marines. NATO forces simulated and reacted to a crisis in western Greece using maritime surface, mine counter-measure and mounted air operations required to support amphibious operations. It is no coincidence, perhaps, that the manoeuvring took place just 150 miles and thirty minutes' flying time from the arid coast of North Africa.

'Dynamic Mix' proved timely. Despite its defeat in the Gulf War, Iraq continued to present the biggest obstacle to peace in the Gulf region. Early in 1998 matters once again reached crisis point with Saddam Hussein's continued refusal to allow UN weapons inspectors to investigate his burgeoning chemical warfare plants. By March, US and Royal Navy forces, including the 6th Fleet of thirty-two ships plus the carriers *George Washington* and *Enterprise*, were once again ready to begin attacks deep in Iraq should diplomacy fail.

Above: Taking off for the return to NAS Sigonella is equally hair-raising, if not more so. The Greyhound moves to the starboard bow cat and, like a butterfly emerging from its chrysalis, stretches out its folded 29ft 4in. wings to their full 80ft 7in. span. Its massive gear is tethered to the starboard bow cat prior to hurtling, projectile fashion, off the forward deck at 150mph in *two* seconds, by a combination of the two massive 4,910ehp Allisons and the steam catapult. The distance to the bow does not look nearly long enough! (*Author*)

Below: Heart-thumping apprehension mounts. *Waaaa . . . mmm!* There is the faint sound of a whipcrack, and then *whoosh . . .!* the Greyhound is propelled into the air with such ferocity that the passengers, sitting facing the rear, arms crossed over their chests, heads down as if saying their prayers, are lifted out of their seats momentarily by the full force of negative G, powerless to do anything except look stupidly at the floor until the G subsides. If their seat belts are not fastened tightly, they will hit the seat in front with such force that they will break teeth and even their jaw. (The two pilots, who fortunately are facing the *right* way, train to withstand 9G.) A slight dip, and '53' is en route for another well-earned shore leave with cargo, passengers and mail. (*Author*)

Above: All hands on deck! Hundreds of busy deck handlers wearing coloured 'float-coats' (snap-on life vests designed to inflate on contact with the water) and 'cranials' (three-piece hard hats with built-in ear protectors and goggles) accomplish various tasks. Purple-coated 'deckies' fuel the aircraft; blue-coated plane handlers disengage chocks and chains from tethered aircraft; red-coated ordnancemen load bombs, rockets, missiles and gun ammunition onto aircraft; green-coated maintainers carry out work on the catapults and the planes; and flight directors, in yellow coats, guide the aircraft to their positions. (*Author*)

Below: Crash Salvage personnel in fire-resistant clothing stand by on deck with their white tractor containing fire extinguishers and hoses. Apart from enemy action, fire is probably the single most dangerous and potentially disastrous calamity that can happen on board a carrier. (*Author*)

Above: A red-coated ordnanceman attends to the port AIM-9L/M Sidewinder IR-homing missile as other ordnancemen and a green-jacketed maintainer (aircraft and catapult) of VF-14 direct a 'Tophatter' Tomcat along the deck after landing.
(*Author*)

Above right: Shortly after being trapped, 'Fly 1' signals an EA-6B Prowler, a fearsome, long, grey beast which carries four tons of electronic warfare equipment, to proceed, and obediently it crosses the deck like a tamed alien predator.
(*Author*)

Below: Looking like volleyball or field hockey players in their 'team strips', or, perhaps more appropriately with their outsize helmets and goggles, pro footballers ready for a gruelling second quarter, deck handlers go about their tasks in front of VFA-87's and VFA-15's F/A-18C Hornets. Sweat and tears mixed with brute force and energy, but above all professionalism, pride and experience, ensure that everything runs 'ship shape and Bristol fashion', as they used to say in Nelson's navy.
(*Author*)

Above: Just after his sortie, a weary but cheerful VFA-87 'Golden Warriors' pilot walks to his debrief. (*Author*)

Below: A VFA-15 'Valions' F/A-18C Hornet carrying centreline and underwing fuel tanks and LAU-10 rocket launchers taxies by the waist cats where a VF-41 'Black Aces' F-14A Tomcat and an F/A-18C of VFA-87 'Golden Warriors' in front of a raised JBD await launching. The 'Golden Warriors' and the 'Valions' are homeported at NAS Cecil Field, Jacksonville, Florida. Both squadrons took part in 'Desert Storm', flying missions as part of CVW-8 on board the USS *Theodore Roosevelt*. (*Author*)

Above: Chain gang. Deck crew cast their long shadows on the waist deck, which is dotted with tie-down spots used for chaining the planes, while brown-coated plane captains confer. Their task is to help aviators get strapped in and make last-minute inspections before take-off, and when they return to assist the weary tailhookers and check over their aircraft so that they are ready for another sortie. (*Author*)

Right: A VF-41 'Black Aces' plane captain climbs into Modex 112 while ordnance personnel gather beneath the barrel and breach air intake troughs of the nose-mounted M61A-1 Vulcan 20mm cannon. This gun gas purge system replaces the earlier, larger but less effective, slatted vents arrangement beneath the cockpit. Both the Tomcat pilot and his WIO sit in tandem on a Martin Baker rocket-assisted, zero-zero GRU7A NACES (Navy Aircrew Common Ejection Seat) under a one-piece bubble canopy that hinges at the rear and gives an excellent all-round view.
(*Author*)

Below: EA-6B Prowler 161352 of VAQ-141 'Shadowhawks' prepares to be catapulted off. The crew comprises a pilot and three ECM officers. ECMO 1 in the forward starboard station provides navigation duties and works the Raytheon AN/ALQ-99F deception jamming system, while ECMOs 3 and 4 in the rear compartment work the AN/ALQ99 TJS (Tactical Jamming System). The small prong at the base of the refuelling probe, and the fairing at the base of the large tailfin pod (which houses the main SIR (System Integration Receivers) antennas to detect enemy radars), house the ALQ-126 DECM (Deception ECM) system which interrupts and confuses enemy radars. Externally, up to four AGM-88A HARM anti-radiation missiles can be carried below the wings, together with AN/ALQ-99 emitter pods, or Aero-1D 300 US gallon drop tanks. A further AN/ALQ-99 pod is carried on the centreline pylon. To reduce the load on the Prowler's electrical generating system, each pod has its own generator driven by a ram air turbine on the nose of the pod. Once, the pods were designed to jam a specific waveband, but the new ICAP-2 (increased capability) version has pods which can jam in any two of seven wavebands.
(*Author*)

Above: A carrier is like a city that never sleeps. This teeming metropolis is always on station and every one of its 5,222 inhabitants has a key function to perform, whether they are 'deckies' responsible for the aircraft, or one of the mess crews who prepare 15,666 meals every day when the Air Wing is embarked. To reach the myriad store rooms, post offices, ablutions, chapel, barber shops, operating theatres, the hangar deck, living accommodation, PX, offices and messes (you name it, the ship has it), you have to hike up and down and along miles and miles of labyrinthine corridors and narrow companionways, passable only by one person at a time. Having the stamina of a mountain goat is an asset. Secreted away in the bowels of this seemingly bottomless ship are ready rooms for each of the nine squadrons embarked. This inner sanctum, home to HS-3 'Tridents', has PCs and a TV, which not only airs movies and news but covers the happenings on deck, day and night, and its walls are adorned with squadron colours, photos and memorabilia, a feature of all ready rooms. Up top can be heard the muffled blasts of aircraft engines, the thump-thump-thump of straining catapults, and chafing arrester wires returning to their starting blocks as one after another aircraft are fired off, or are recovered. HS-3 fly Sikorsky SH-60F Ocean Hawk and HH-60H Seahawk crews (Cdr John 'Saddam' Husaim, left, and Lt Wayne 'Gooch' Gutierrez, centre). The SH-60F is the Navy's CV Inner Zone anti-submarine helicopter to protect the CBG (Carrier Battle Group) from close-in enemy submarines. The HH-60H is a combat SAR and special support helicopter. (*Author*)

Below and following page : USS *John F. Kennedy* sailing in the Mediterranean with CVW-8 on board. President Kennedy's daughter Caroline, the ship's sponsor, christened and launched the carrier on 27 May 1967. Entering naval service on 7 September 1968, 'Big John' has spent much of her career in the Mediterranean, completing fourteen deployments by 1993. On 16 January 1991, aircraft from the ship's Carrier Air Wing Three began Operation 'Desert Storm' with attacks on Iraqi forces. *Kennedy* launched 114 strikes and 2,895 sorties, with the aircrews of CVW-3, mainly from the Red Sea, flying 11,263 combat hours and delivering more than 3,500,000lb of ordnance in the conflict, during which CVW-3 made the first operational use of the SLAM missile. On 13 September 1995 'Big John' completed a two-year $491 billion comprehensive overhaul at the Philadelphia Naval Shipyard, which has extended the life of the carrier by another eight to nine years. (*Author*)

Left: An EA-6B Prowler of VAQ-141 'Shadowhawks' folds its wings after landing. In the foreground is a VF-41 'Black Aces' F-14A and a C-2A of VRC-40 'Rawhides'. VRC-40 (Fleet Tactical Support Squadron), previously known as 'Codfish Airlines', was established on 1 July 1960 and operates the Greyhound for COD support in the Atlantic fleet. VR-24 (Fleet Logistic Support Squadron) 'Lifting Eagles', which calls itself 'The Biggest Little Airline', also carries out transport duties with C-2A and CT-39G Sabreliner aircraft for carriers in the Mediterranean from NAS Sigonella in Sicily.
(*Author*)

Below and following page: An E-2C Hawkeye of VAW-124 'Bear Aces' carrying more than six tons of electronic equipment, and three radar operators facing sideways, is trapped before moving away. At first glance the E-2C looks as if it was put together by a committee. However, the designers did not want the vertical fins to obstruct the radar signals, though they wanted a lot of fin area in case the plane has to land with one engine shut down, so four fins, three of them carrying tandem-hinged rudders, were used. To reduce radar interference, specially developed Hamilton-Standard four-bladed props have fibreglass skins over a foam core on a solid aluminium spar. For easy storage, the Hawkeye's wings twist and fold backwards, while the rotodome can be lowered hydraulically. Like the C-2A, the E-2 is the only aircraft that operates from the deck of a ship that does not have rocket-powered ejection seats.
(*Author*)

Above: An S-3B is catapulted off the waist cat of the *Kennedy*. The Viking, or 'Hoover', as it is known because of the sound emitted from its high-bypass-ratio General Electric TF34 turbofans, first flew on 21 January 1972, and entered service in February 1974 with VS-41 'Shamrocks' at NAS North Island, San Diego, California. (*Author*)

Below: An ES-3A Shadow of VQ-6 (Fleet Air Reconnaissance squadron) 'Ravens' and an S-3B Viking of VS-24 (Sea-Control Squadron 24) 'Scouts' get ready to be catapulted off the waist cats on board *Kennedy*, the first carrier to take the S-3 to sea, in 1975. The ES-3A is the newest edition to the Navy's Carrier Wings, providing the battle group with electronic surveillance (ELINT), including intercept of enemy communications (COMINT). Height from the keel to the mast top on the 'island' *behind* is the same as a twenty-three-storey building. (*Author*)

Above: An S-3B of VS-24 gets airborne from the bow catapult. VS-24, which was established on 25 May 1960, is homeported at NAS Cecil Field, Jacksonville, Florida. During 'Desert Storm' the 'Scouts', part of CVW-8 on board the *Theodore Roosevelt*, operated as 'ground attack Vikings' armed with Mk 82 500lb bombs and other ordnance, flying bombing missions against Iraqi ground as well as sea targets. (*Author*)

Below: S-3B Viking of VS-24 'Scouts' snags the arrester wire but completes its mission, much to the satisfaction of 'Fly 1'. Each wire has a tensile strength of 176,000lb. Regular checks are made to make sure that they are not about to snap. After 100 'traps', a wire is removed and thrown overboard to ensure that it is never mistakenly fitted and used again. (*Author*)

Above: Final approach for Tomcat pilots is usually flown with a sink rate of 750 feet per minute, and this is calculated to bring the F-14 down to engage the third of the four arrester wires. Its attitude at this stage of the flight has acquired for it the dubious nickname of 'turkey' ('cause everything is hanging down)! (*Author*)

Below: A lightly loaded Hornet can be launched without using afterburner, though this F/A-18C of VFA-15 'Valions' leaves the bow of the *Kennedy* on full re-heat. From zero to 160 knots in four seconds, it is pulling about 4G as it zooms into the air. The two General Electric F404-GE-402 afterburning low-bypass turbofans are rated at about 16,000lb, more than useful when hauling a normal take-off load of 36,710lb for a typical fighter mission, or 49,224lb for an attack mission. (*Author*)

Above: The arrester hook takes a fifty-ton load when the wire is engaged. As soon as the twenty-two-ton aircraft slams onto the deck (placing an eighty-ton load on the undercarriage, thirty tons on the nosewheel, and each ton of stores a ten-ton load), the Tomcat pilot (who along with his RIO has just absorbed a one-and-a-half-ton load) has to open the throttles to full power in case he has to 'bolter'. This occurs when the arrester wires are missed and he is forced to power out on a touch-and-go.
(*Author*)

Below: A Tomcat's great 64ft 1½in. wing with flaps extending across the full span are an enormous aid to recovery. The aircraft is typically trapped at 130 knots or less on landing and the F-14 comes to a dead stop from its approach speed in only two seconds. Even so, to the casual bystander, the aircraft appears *every* time to finish menacingly close to the end of the ramp!
(*Author*)

Above: A flight director motions away Modex 202, a 'Tophatters' F-14A, immediately after landing. The nose of the F-14A houses the Hughes AWG-9 radar and fire-control system which is capable of picking out and tracking low-flying aircraft against ground or sea clutter. The chin housing accommodates an ECM antenna in the lower section and the cylindrical casing above contains a Northrop AXX-1 stabilised telephoto video camera (TV Camera Set (TCS) with a range in excess of ten miles) which is steered by the radar. (*Author*)

Below: 'Fighting 31' has the famous 'Felix the cat and bomb' emblem, and 'Fighting 84' has inherited the equally historic 'Jolly Rogers' skull and crossbones, but when VF-14, as befits the oldest squadron in the Navy, with a continuous history stretching back to 1919, adds the unique black topper, and a tux, to the universal grinning tomcat and stars logo, it really takes the cream. (*Author*)

Above: Warm winter sunshine glistens on the calm Mediterranean as Tomcats and Hornets are manhandled and repositioned on deck just like a huge chess game. During operational deployments scores of aircraft have to be moved, on time and in sequence, for maximum efficiency and optimum storage space, so every manoeuvre is carefully thought out and choreographed in flight operations using two-dimensional plastic aircraft on a model deck.
(Author)

Above: A relatively calm interlude ensues between launchings and recoveries, but it's really only an illusion, for a few feet away the rare respite from activity is filled with a valuable opportunity to search the deck (below), and nooks and crannies for loose items that cause Foreign Object Damage (FOD). A few cents' worth of FOD, when sucked into an engine, can easily ground a multi-million-dollar jet. (*Author*)

Above: Recoveries and launchings are coming to a close, and this F/A-18C is lowered on one of the four 4,000-square-feet elevators aboard to be neatly stowed in the vast hangar deck below for any maintenance problems or 'gripes' that will need attending to during the night. (*Author*)

Above: Quality Check personnel strike up a pose beside an F/A-18C Hornet of VFA-15 'Valions' at the end of another long but rewarding day. The average age of sailors on board is just nineteen and their motivation is a beacon for all to see.
(*Author*)

Above: It is amazing how easily Tomcats and Hornets, with their folding wings swept back or tips raised skywards, can be so neatly spotted and densely packed amidst the contours and confines of a modern carrier, without hindrance to operational take-offs and landings. Then, when operations finally cease, they will, like slaves from the days of galleons, be chained to the deck of the ship on which they sail.
(*Author*)

CHAPTER 7
FANTAILS

Below: Since 1946 more than 217 million people have watched the Navy Flight Demonstration Squadron, the Blue Angels. Each demonstration represents hundreds of hours of practice, maintenance and support efforts on the part of seven jet pilots, three transport pilots, the squadron Naval Flight Officer, five staff officers and almost eighty enlisted men and women. Each year the NFDS selects about three tactical jet pilots, three staff officers and a Marine Corps C-130 transport pilot. Each Blue Angel demonstration pilot will have flown more than 1,500 hours in a tactical jet and had a tour aboard a carrier. The Blue Angels replaced its A-4Fs in 1986 and began training with F/A-18s that winter. This display at MacDill AFB, Florida was photographed by Graham Dinsdale in September 1996.

Below: These commitments extended to 'keeping the Bear at bay' in Europe and the Mediterranean. On this occasion, an F-4S Phantom of VF-74 'Bedevilers' maintains a close, careful watch on a high-flying Tupolev Tu-20 'Bear'. In 1983 Fighting Seven Four replaced its Phantoms with the F-14A Tomcat.
(*USN*)

130

Below: A tailhookers' approach view of the 1,000-foot steel runway of the 82,000-ton USS *John F. Kennedy* cruising west of Crete. Object of the exercise is to catch the third of the four arrester wires in the barren area of the 4.56-acre deck, denoted by the worn-away white centreline, erased by the constant impact of numerous landings. The angled flight deck, which allows free take-off and landing of aircraft without the need to protect parked aircraft (some of whose tails appear to hang precariously over the side) with a crash barrier is, like the steam catapult, a British invention to cater for fast-jet operation. Two of the three octuple Mk 29 launchers for RIM-7 Sea Sparrow SAM missiles can be seen on the stern at either edge of the flight deck (the third is situated on a sponson on the starboard forward deck). The two white domes left of the deck contain the two SPN-42 landing radars, while the thimble white radome is one of three which surmount the 20mm Phalanx Mk 15 close-in weapon system. The opening, or fantail, in the stern is used for testing aircraft engines. (*Author*)

Above: An S-3B Viking of VS-24 'Scouts' taking off from the waist cat aboard the USS *John F. Kennedy*. (*Author*)

Above: Keeping watch. Aboard the USS *George Washington*, 17 February 1998, Carrier Air Wing One (CVW-1) LSOs evaluate an ES-3A 'Shadow' landing on board. CVW-1 and the *George Washington* were deployed to the Persian Gulf in support of Operation 'Southern Watch'.
(*USN photo by Photographer's Mate 3rd Class Brian Fleske*)

Opposite: Sunset over the Med from Beech UC-12M 163841, one of eleven Super King Airs used by the USN for liaison and communications.
(*Author*)

Above: A VF-41 'Black Aces' F-14A Tomcat getting airborne from the deck of the USS *John F. Kennedy*. (*Author*)

Above: Crash Salvage personnel onboard *John F. Kennedy* at work and rest. (*Author*)

Below: Evocative shot of an F-14 Tomcat coming into land aboard its carrier. (*The Aviation workshop*)

Above: F-14 Tomcat taking on fuel from its refuelling tanker. (*The Aviation Workshop*)

Above: AW2 Bryan Norcross of HS-3 'Tridents' from the *Kennedy* keeps watch through the open doorway of the HH-60H Seahawk during a sortie over the Mediterranean. (*Author*)

Above: View from a bridge, or from the flag bridge at the 08 level on the island to be precise. The original superstructure of the USS *John F. Kennedy* was far simpler and less cluttered than it is today. The blue-coated operator is kneeling on the roof of the camera station on the 07 level.

Above is the navigation bridge at the 09 level and jutting out is Pr-Fly on the top 010 level where the air boss and mini boss control air operations from their large chairs. (*Author*)

Above: Airman from Carrier Air Wing Eight walking the deck.
(*Author*)

Above: White-coated and brown-coated VAQ-141 'Shadowhawks' personnel onboard *Kennedy*.
(*Author*)

INDEX